for the
Busy Bride
on a Budget!

HOT
OFF THE
PRESS INC.

Designers:

LeNae Gerig

LeNae Gerig lives in Oregon with her husband Chris, their daughter Lauren, and their dog Bailey. LeNae is an in-house designer, scrapbook specialist and technical editor for Hot Off The Press; she's written and contributed to nearly a hundred books and has planned dozens of weddings.

Dedicated to my friend and sister-in-law, Keri Gerig Hoffman, for all the babysitting. Thanks!

Kathy Thompson

Kathy Thompson lives in Oregon with her husband, Rick, and their two sons. Kathy is a professional florist and has designed over 30 books for Hot Off The Press.

Models:

Laura Bush
Sarah Daniels
Lauren Gerig
Keri Hoffman
Mercedes Lorenzo

Sara Naumann
Amanda Parsons
Krystal Peterson
Joy Schaber

Hairdresser:

Ana Worley

Thank you to the following churches:

Canby Christian Church, Oregon
Elliott Prairie Community Church, Oregon

Production Credits:

President: Paulette Jarvey
Vice President: Teresa Nelson
Production Manager: Lynda Hill
Editors: Teresa Nelson, Lynda Hill
Project Editor: Sherry Harbert
Technical Editors: LeNae Gerig, Arlene Peterson
Photographer: John McNally
Graphic Designers: Joy Schaber, Jacie Pete
Digital Imagers: Victoria Weber, Larry Seith, Gretchen Putman

published by:

HOT OFF THE PRESS INC.

For a color catalog of nearly 800 products, send $2.00 to:

HOT OFF THE PRESS INC.
1250 N.W. Third, Dept. B
Canby, Oregon 97013
phone (503) 266-9102
1-800-227-9595
fax (503) 266-8749
http://www.craftpizazz.com

for the
Busy Bride
on a Budget!

Table of Contents

Table of Contents

Bridal Florals 56-95

Decorating for the Ceremony 96-121

Reception Decorations 122-139

Tips & Patterns 140-143

Bridal Bows & Basics

A wedding is a wonderful celebration and it's a natural for each of us to want our special event to be extraordinary, filled with our own distinctive tastes and touches. While the flurry and excitement of preparing for a wedding can be thrilling, those preparations can also result in hectic days and unwanted bills. This book can help eliminate some of those frantic times and many of those bills. Although some expenses can't be avoided, here are many choices in bridal accessories, decorating ideas and florals for the entire wedding party, which can bring substantial relief to your budget.

One wedding item representing the most savings is the bridal headpiece. Tulle veils, gorgeous flowers, pearl sprays, lace appliques and other bridal materials are found in most craft stores and can be assembled easily with a bit of wire and glue. As a result, hundreds of dollars can be saved while creating a customized headpiece that is perfect for you.

This book is filled with instructions for decorating nearly everything in the wedding, from the facility being used to the entire wedding party—and because you're making the items yourself, you'll save money while creating exactly the look and feeling you want for your special day!

Let's begin with some basic information, including instructions for making bows and tips for working with floral materials. While directions for creating the pieces are complete, please feel free to change and customize your wedding so it represents you perfectly. Most of all, have fun creating the wedding of your dreams!

Bridal Bows & Basics

Wiring & Taping Stems:

1 Separate the floral sprigs by cutting them off the stem in the desired lengths.

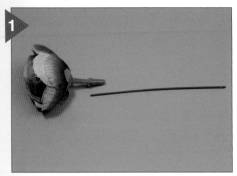

2 Hold the wire length next to the sprig stem; place one end of the floral tape on the wire next to the cluster. Wrap the tape around the stem and wire, stretching it as you wrap downward. At the end, pull and stretch the tape to tear it, then press the end onto the taped stem to secure it.

Working with Dried Millet:

Carefully hold the millet stems over a pan of boiling water to make them more pliable for bending. Bend and wire as directed, then let them air-dry completely.

dried millet stems

Helpful Hint

Working with florals is easier than you think! If you're unsure of an insertion position for a particular stem, first insert it into the foam without applying glue. Once you're sure of the placement, pull it out, apply glue and reinsert it.

Working with Bouquet Holders:

Bouquet holders are available in most craft stores and florist shops. Simply insert your floral stems into the caged foam base of the holder, making sure it's oriented in the same direction as you fill it.

bouquet holder with foam cage

Working with Rose Petals:

Gently pull the petals from roses in full bloom; discard any petals with brown edges. Place each on a sheet of newspaper and allow to air dry for a week. Try to avoid humid areas. Lavender dries nicely, too; and makes a nice aromatic additon to the favors.

dried lavender and rose petals

Working with Stems & Sprigs:

A *stem* refers to the entire stem of flowers as purchased. When cut apart, the individual pieces become *sprigs*.

stem length

sprigs cut from the stem

sprig length

stem length

When a *length* is given, measure from the blossom tip to the stem end.

When a *sprig length* is given, measure it from the blossom tip to the stem end. If the *stem length* is given, measure the stem from the end to just under the blossom.

How to Make a Dior Bow:

1 Cut a 3", 9", 11" and 12" length of ribbon. Form the 12" length into a circle.

2 Pinch the center to make a bow shape.

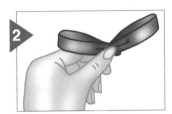

3 Center the 9" and 11" lengths under the bow for tails and wire together in the center. Wrap the 3" length over the center wire and glue the ends in the back. Cut each tail diagonally.

How to Make a Loopy Bow:

1 Measure the desired tail length from the end of the ribbon and make a loop on each side of your thumb.

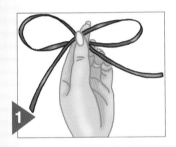

2 Continue making loops on each side of your thumb until the desired number is reached; (if you need an eight-loop bow, make four loops on each side).

3 Wrap the center with wire and twist tightly at the back to secure; trim the wire ends. Or secure the bow by wrapping ribbon around the center and tying it in the back, which adds a second set of tails. Cut each tail diagonally.

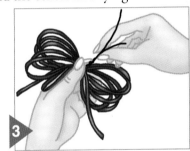

How to Make a Puffy Bow:

1 Beginning with one ribbon end, make the center loop.

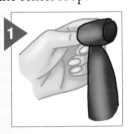

2 Make a loop on one side of your thumb. Give the ribbon a twist and make another loop on the other side of your thumb. Continue making loops and twists until the desired number is reached, (a ten-loop bow has five loops on each side).

3 Make one large loop for the tails. Insert a wire through the center loop; bring the ends to the back and twist securely. Cut the long loop diagonally, as shown.

How to Make a Shoestring Bow:

1 Measure the desired tail length from the end of the ribbon, then make a loop of the specified length. Wrap the free end of the ribbon loosely around the center of the bow.

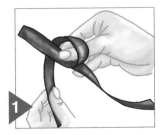

2 Form a loop in the free end of the ribbon and push it through the center loop. Pull the loops in opposite directions to tighten, then pull on the tails to adjust the size of the loops. Trim each tail diagonally or in an inverted "V".

Melissa Michaels

Tawnya Phyllis Orr
and
...n Robert Langendorfer
...ether with their parents
... Mrs. Andrew R. Orr
and
...rs. Robert G. Langendorfer
...you to share in the
...ir new life together
...hange marriage vows
...the second of May
...d and ninety-eight
...in the evening
...ncer Chapel
...Oregon
...owing at
...Town Hall

Cassandra Lyn Walters
And
Christopher Jay Moore
along with our parents
request the honor of your presence
at our marriage
on Saturday, the twenty-eighth of July
Two Thousand and one
At eleven o'clock in the morning
Salem Catholic Church
Salem, Massachusetts
Lunch reception
Immediately following the ceremony

Cassandra Lyn Walters and Christopher Jay Moore
Are happy to announce their marriage
On Saturday, the twenty-eighth of July
Two Thousand and one
At Eleven o'clock in the morning
In Salem, Massachusetts

Please mark your calendars and save this date
For more information on travel and hotels
Please see our web site at www.gettinghittched.com

Wendy and Todd

April and Jon

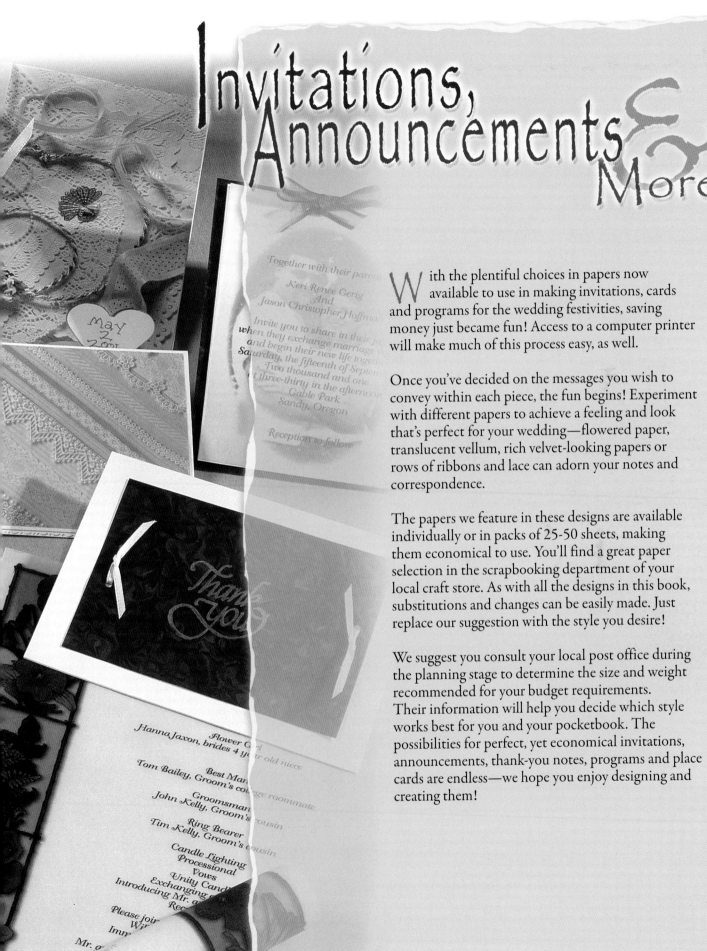

Invitations, Announcements & More

With the plentiful choices in papers now available to use in making invitations, cards and programs for the wedding festivities, saving money just became fun! Access to a computer printer will make much of this process easy, as well.

Once you've decided on the messages you wish to convey within each piece, the fun begins! Experiment with different papers to achieve a feeling and look that's perfect for your wedding—flowered paper, translucent vellum, rich velvet-looking papers or rows of ribbons and lace can adorn your notes and correspondence.

The papers we feature in these designs are available individually or in packs of 25-50 sheets, making them economical to use. You'll find a great paper selection in the scrapbooking department of your local craft store. As with all the designs in this book, substitutions and changes can be easily made. Just replace our suggestion with the style you desire!

We suggest you consult your local post office during the planning stage to determine the size and weight recommended for your budget requirements. Their information will help you decide which style works best for you and your pocketbook. The possibilities for perfect, yet economical invitations, announcements, thank-you notes, programs and place cards are endless—we hope you enjoy designing and creating them!

THANK YOU

With great thankfulness to God
Amy Evelyn Smith
and
Jack Stephan Chandler
invite you to share in their joy
as they unite in marriage
and begin their life together
Saturday, the fifteenth of May
...o thousand and one
...ck in the afternoon
...ngelical Free Church
...y, Oregon
...n to follow

Sam, Kerry, tina
and John

Please do us the favor
Of responding by
April 30, 2001
Name_____
Number of Adults_____
Unable to attend_____

Set by LeNae Gerig

The paper set shown above has a very contemporary look, so it's best to use a style of type (called a font) that fits with the swirl theme. Try to avoid heavy letters or those that look "Old World." Once you've chosen the one you like, use it throughout your wedding materials. A font works in much the same way as your color scheme, therefore consistency is important.

Lavender Swirl Invitation

Paper Pizazz® purple sponged paper
Paper Pizazz® swirl vellum paper
Paper Flair™ 2 Envelopes Template
Paper Flair™ 5"x6½" white blank card & envelope
2" wide swirl stamp
lavender stamp pad
1" wide swirl punch
straight-edged scissors
pencil
glue stick
computer and printer

1 Type your invitation text on the computer using your chosen font, and center it to fit within a 5"x6½" space. Cut a blank card in half along the fold line. Hand feed one half into your printer.

2 Place the printed card face up on a scrap piece of paper. Ink the stamp and stamp around the border of the card, rotating the stamp as you progress around the card; let it dry thoroughly. Hand-write your addess and place a postage stamp on the white envelope front for your recipient to return the response card (see next column).

3 Lightly trace the large envelope template onto the vellum paper with a pencil; cut it out. Fold and glue the envelope following the directions on the template.

4 Place the invitation (and response card) face down on the addressed side of the white return envelope and insert both into the vellum envelope; seal the envelope with the glue stick. Punch a swirl from the sponged paper and glue it centered on the back edge of the flap. Address the vellum envelope front to your recipient and add postage as usual.

Helpful Hint

Announcements *are sent to everyone, while* **invitations** *are sent just to those you wish to invite to the wedding ceremony and reception. A* **response card** *is sent with the invitation to gather specific numbers attending the events. Make sure you hand-write each individual name you wish to invite, to avoid unexpected arrivals.*

Lavender Swirl Response Card

Paper Flair™ 5"x6½" white blank card & envelope
2" wide swirl stamp
lavender stamp pad
lavender pen
straight-edged scissors
computer and printer

1 Type your response text, on the computer using your chosen font, and center it to fit within a 4"x6" space. Cut a blank card to 4"x6". Hand feed it into your printer.

2 Ink the swirl stamp and stamp once in the upper right corner of the card. With the lavender pen, draw the squiggle and dot pattern (below) along the four edges of the card. At the top of the card, hand-write the name of each guest invited.

3 Insert the response card next to the return envelope with the invitation.

Lavender Swirl "Thank You" Card

Paper Pizazz® purple sponged paper
Paper Flair™ 5"x6½" white blank card & envelope
black paper
2" wide swirl stamp
lavender stamp pad
straight-edged scissors
glue stick
computer and printer

1 Type "Thank You", on the computer using your chosen font, and center it to fit within a 4¼"x3½" rectangle, adding as many rectangles as possible on a letter-sized page. Print it out on purple sponged paper and cut out the rectangles, centering each phrase.

2 Mat the rectangle on black paper, leaving a ⅛" border. With the card fold at the top, ink the stamp and stamp four patterns along the bottom edge of the card front. Glue the "Thank You" centered ½" below the fold on the card front.

3 Open the envelope flap face up on a sheet of scrap paper. Ink the stamp and stamp swirls to cover the flap. Address and add postage to the front as usual.

Welcome to the Wedding of Cassandra and Christopher

Maid of Honor: Molly Jackson, Groom's sister
Bride's Maids: Karen Keen, Bride's cousin
Sydney Cline, Bride's friend for 22 years
Julie Atkins, Bride's college roommate
Junior Bride's Maid: Sara Jackson, Bride's niece
Flower Girl: Victoria Jackson, Bride's niece

Best Man: ... Maxwell, Groom's cousin
Groom's M... ...ell, Groom's college roommate
...room's cousin
...riend of Groom
...nell, Groom's c...

Cassandra Lyn Walters and Christopher Jay Moore
Are happy to announce their marriage
On Saturday, the twenty-eighth of July
Two Thousand and one
At Eleven o'clock in the morning
In Salem, Massachusetts

Please mark your calendars and save this date
For more information on travel and hotel...

THANK YOU

Cassandra Lyn Walters

And

Christopher Jay Moore

along with our parents

request the honor of your presence
at our marriage

on Saturday, the twenty-eighth of July
Two Thousand and one
At eleven o'clock in the morning

Salem Catholic Church
Salem, Massachusetts

Lunch reception
Immediately following the ceremony

Set by LeNae Gerig

This set carries the traditional look, but adds a modern touch. It includes a "Save the Date" card, an addition to your announcement package to give those who live farther away time to plan for travel and accommodations. Send these cards at least three months in advance, realizing they don't preclude the invitations. Those are sent to every invited guest within a reasonable time period before the wedding.

Pink Roses "Save the Date" Card

Paper Pizazz® muted roses and pink moiré papers
Paper Flair™ 5"x6½" white blank card & envelope
9" of ⅜" wide sheer white ribbon with satin edges
straight-edged scissors
ruler
glue stick
computer and printer

1 Type your announcement text, on the computer in landscape mode using your chosen font, and center it to fit within a 4¾"x2⅞" space. Copy the entire text and place it 3 more times on the page; making sure to provide space between each text block. Print it out on pink moiré and cut each sheet into four 4¾"x2⅞" pieces.

2 Glue one announcement piece centered on a 3⅞"x5⅜" rectangle of the roses paper. Cut the card in half along the fold line. Glue the roses piece centered on one of the card halves. Tie the ribbon into a shoestring bow (see page 9) and glue it above the pink moiré.

Pink Roses "Thank You" Card

Paper Pizazz® muted roses paper
Paper Pizazz® pink moiré paper
Paper Flair™ 5"x6½" white blank card & envelope
white paper
straight-edged scissors
ruler
pencil
glue stick
computer and printer

1 Cut off 2" along the right open side of the card front. Cut a 2¾"x6¼" rectangle from the roses paper; glue it centered on the remaining card front. Cut a 4¾"x6¼" rectangle from the pink moiré; open the card and glue it centered to the inside back.

2 Type "Thank You" on the computer to fit a 2⅜"x1⅞" rectangle and print it out on white paper. Mat it on pink moiré, leaving a ⅛" border; mat it again on white, leaving a 1/16" border. Glue the matted "Thank You" centered on the card front, with the right side extending 1" beyond the right edge of the card front.

Pink Roses Invitation

Paper Pizazz® pink moiré paper
Paper Pizazz® vellum ferns paper
white cardstock
9" of ⅜" wide sheer white ribbon with satin edges
straight-edged scissors
ruler
pencil
glue stick
computer and printer

1 Type your invitation text on the computer, centered to fit a 3¼"x8¼" space; copy the text and place it once more on the page. Print it on the pink moiré, then cut each to a 3¼"x8¼" rectangle.

2 Cut the cardstock into two 3½"x8⅜" rectangles. Glue the printed moiré centered on the card stock. Tie the ribbon into a shoestring bow (see page 9) and glue it above the printed text on the moiré.

3 **For the envelope:** with a pencil, lightly trace the pattern onto the vellum paper. Fold the left and right sides to the center using the dotted lines in the pattern. Glue the overlapping edges together. Fold the bottom flap up and glue to secure. Place the 3½"x8⅜" blank card stock over the invitation text and insert both pieces into the envelope. Fold the envelope top flap down and glue to secure. Address and add postage to the front of the envelope to mail.

Pink Roses Program

Paper Pizazz® muted roses paper
Paper Pizazz® pink moiré paper
7" of ⅜" wide white satin ribbon with sheer edges
⅛" wide hole punch
straight-edged scissors
ruler, pencil, glue stick
computer and printer

Type your program text on the computer, centering it to fit a 7"x9½" space. Print it on the pink moiré. Place a dab of glue in the center of the muted roses paper, then place the printed moiré centered on top. Punch two holes ½" apart above the printing on the moiré. Thread the ribbon through the holes from the back and tie it in a double knot.

invitation envelope

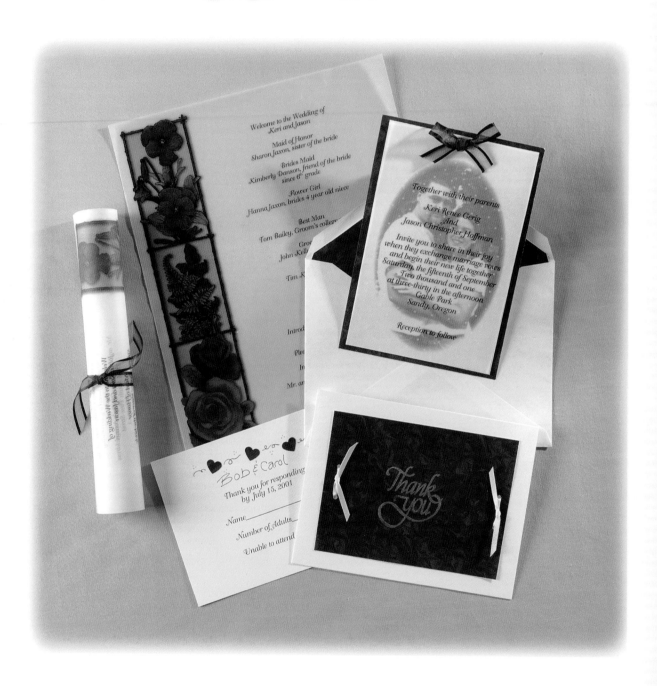

Set by LeNae Gerig

Because of the formality of this set, a traditional style of type (called a font) looks pretty on these pieces. The wedding program is printed on floral and ferns four-color vellum paper and is rolled to become a keepsake for each guest. Vellum adds an elegant touch and the four-color designs will make your program look spectacular.

Burgundy Invitation

Paper Pizazz® 12"x12" burgundy suede printed paper
Paper Pizazz® vellum dots paper
Paper Flair™ 5"x6½" white blank card & envelope
9" of ⅜" wide burgundy sheer ribbon with satin edges
1/16" wide hole punch
engagement photo
straight-edged scissors
pencil
glue stick
computer with digital photo program and printer

1 Use a digital image of the couple to create the photo effects you want, using the computer. Center it within a 3¾"x5¼" space, using a soft edge border. Cut the card to 4½"x6⅜" rectangle and hand-feed each card through the printer.

2 Type your invitation text, on the computer using your chosen font, and center it to fit within a 4½"x6⅜" space. Copy the entire text and place it three more times on the page, making sure to provide space between each text block. Print it out on the vellum dots paper and cut it into four pieces. Place one printed vellum piece over the photo; punch two holes 1" apart near the top. Thread the ribbon through the holes from the back and tie in a shoestring bow (see page 9). Glue the card to a 4¾"x6⅞" piece of the printed burgundy suede paper.

3 Open the envelope flap onto the printed suede paper; trace around it, extending the bottom edge 7" from the flap point, and decreasing the sides by ½". Cut it out and insert it into the envelope face up ⅜" from the envelope flap edge; glue it in place.

Burgundy Program

Paper Pizazz® vellum floral & ferns paper
9" of ⅜" wide burgundy sheer ribbon with satin edges
computer and printer

1 Type your program text, on the computer using your chosen font, and center it to fit to the left of the image on the vellum; print it on the vellum.

2 Roll each sheet into a 1½" wide tube; wrap the ribbon around the center and knot to secure, trimming the ends.

Burgundy Response Card

Paper Pizazz® 12"x12" burgundy suede printed paper
Paper Flair™ 5"x6½" white blank card & envelope
½" wide heart punch
gold pen
black pen
straight edge scissors
glue stick
computer and printer

1 Type your response text, on the computer using your chosen font, and center it to fit within a 4"x6" space. Cut a blank card to 4"x6". Hand-feed each card through the printer.

2 Punch three hearts from the printed suede paper; glue them at random angles centered over the words on the card. With the black pen, draw a looping line on each side of each heart and write the name of each guest invited between the hearts and printed text. With the gold pen, draw six groups of tri-dots around the hearts.

3 Hand-write your adress on the envelope and place postage in the corner for your recipient to return the card. Insert the response card and return envelope with the invitation.

Burgundy "Thank You" Card

Paper Pizazz® 12"x12" burgundy suede printed paper
Paper Flair™ 5"x6½" white blank card & envelope
12" of ⅛" wide white satin ribbon
"Thank You" stamp
metallic gold stamp pad
ruler
straight-edged scissors
glue stick

1 Cut a 5⅜"x4" rectangle from the printed suede paper; glue it centered on the card front. Ink the stamp and stamp the center of the burgundy rectangle.

2 Open the card. Punch two holes, 1" apart and centered on each short side of the burgundy rectangle. Cut the ribbon in half. Thread each piece through the holes from inside the card front and knot to secure.

Set by LeNae Gerig

This classic theme begins with the announcement and carries through the reception. The place cards are perfect for intimate dining or rehearsal dinners. If your guest list is larger than 25, ordering the papers in bulk is recommended. In fact, order extra to be prepared for any last minute additions or changes.

Pearls & Lace Announcement

Paper Pizazz® diagonal ribbons paper
Paper Flair™ 5"x6½" blank white card & envelope
white, ivory, cream papers
9" of ¼" wide ivory satin ribbon
scalloped-edged scissors
straight-edged scissors
ruler, pencil
glue stick
computer and printer

1 Open the card and fold the two outside edges in to meet over the center fold. Cut two 2¼"x6¼" rectangles of the diagonal ribbons paper; glue a piece centered on each front flap.

2 Type your invitation text, on your computer using your chosen font, and making it fit within a 3⅛"x5¼" rectangle. Print it on cream paper, then mat it on ivory, leaving a ¹⁄₁₆" border. Glue it centered on the inside back of the card.

3 Use the same font to print out the first names of the bride and groom to fit in an oval on white paper; cut it out. Mat the oval on ivory, using the patterned-edged scissors to make a ¹⁄₁₆" border. Tie the ribbon into a shoestring bow (see page 9) and glue it to the oval top. Glue the oval centered on the left front flap, extending over the right flap.

Pearls & Lace Place Card

Paper Pizazz® diagonal ribbons paper
white, ivory papers
7" of ½" wide white satin ribbon with sheer edges
straight-edged scissors
ruler
pencil
glue stick
computer and printer

1 Type the name of each guest, on the computer using your chosen font, and making it fit within a 2⅞"x1⁵⁄₁₆" rectangle. Print it on ivory paper, then mat it on white, leaving a ¹⁄₁₆" border.

2 Cut a 3¼"x4¾" rectangle from the diagonal ribbons paper; fold it in half. Glue the matted name plate centered on the front flap. Tie the ribbon in a shoestring bow (see page 9) and glue it centered on the name plate top edge.

Pearls & Lace Program

Paper Pizazz® doilies & charms paper
white paper
24" of ¼" wide ivory satin ribbon
2" wide heart punch
gold pen
computer and printer

1 Type your program text, on the computer using your chosen font, in landscape (long) mode and centering the text in two halves of the page. Print it on white paper, then fold in half.

2 **For the cover:** with the doilies & charms paper turned so the tassels appear in the lower left corner, punch a heart in the lower right corner. Fold it in half. Insert a printed program inside the cover.

3 Write the wedding date on the white paper inside the heart shape with the gold pen, then outline the shape. Wrap the ribbon around the fold of the papers and knot, as shown in the photo.

Pearls & Lace "Thank You" Card

Paper Pizazz® diagonal ribbons paper
Paper Flair™ 5"x6½" blank white card & envelope
2" wide heart punch
gold pen
scalloped-edged scissors
straight-edged scissors
ruler
pencil
glue stick

1 Use the patterned scissors to trim along the long edge of the card's front flap. Use the ruler and pen to draw a gold line just above the patterned edge. Cut a 6¼"x4¼" rectangle of the diagonal ribbons paper; glue it centered to the card front.

2 Punch a heart in the lower left corner of the card front. Write "Thank you" inside the heart shape and outline the heart opening in gold.

Helpful Hint

Hand-writing each envelope is recommended, though there are time-saving alternatives. Use your printer to print the names and addresses. Try to avoid using labels, even in the return address corner.

The Wedding Party by LeNae Gerig

Paper Pizazz® 12"x12" lily and green stripes papers
Paper Pizazz® 12"x12" white, ivory papers
patterned-edged scissors
straight-edged scissors
wavy edge ruler
black pen
ruler and pencil
glue stick

1   Trace the wavy edge ruler across the back of the lily paper, 2" from the lower edge and cut on the line. Cut a 2"x12" strip of white paper and glue it to the back of the lily paper, extending ½" below the wavy line. Cut the excess off, leaving ⅛" beyond the lily paper edge. Cut a 3"x12" strip of the green stripes paper. Glue the lily paper on it, so the page measures 12"x12".

2   Cut the oval from the striped paper; mat it on white, using the patterned scissors to make a ¹⁄₁₆" wide border. Cut out a lily from a scrap and glue it centered on the oval, then glue the oval as shown. With the black pen, journal names and dates on the oval. Crop and mat wedding photos as desired and glue in place.

Portrait of the Bride by LeNae Gerig

Paper Pizazz® 12"x12" green with white dots and green
   flourishes papers
sage green paper
Paper Pizazz® 12"x12" white paper
patterned-edged scissors
straight-edged scissors
ruler and pencil
glue stick

1   Cut both patterned papers to 11" squares; then cut each in half diagonally. Use the straight-edged scissors to cut the dots paper and the patterned scissors to cut the flourishes paper.

2   Position a triangle from each patterned paper onto a 12"x12" sheet of white, leaving a ⅜" between them. Mat a bridal portrait on white, then on sage, leaving a ¹⁄₁₆" border each time. Mat it once more on white, using the patterned scissors to make a ¹⁄₁₆" border, then glue it centered on the page.

The Bridal Shower by LeNae Gerig

Paper Pizazz® 12"x12" pink gingham, green stripes and green diamonds papers
Paper Pizazz® 12"x12" white paper
⅜" wide heart punch
straight-edged scissors
black pen
ruler and pencil
glue stick
tracing paper, transfer paper

1 Cut the green stripes paper to 10¾" square and mat it on white, leaving a ⅛" border. Glue it centered on the green diamonds paper. Transfer the umbrella top pattern (see page 142) to the pink gingham and the handle to white; cut each piece. Mat the umbrella top on white, leaving a 1⁄16" border. Glue the handle and top together as shown, then journal on the top.

2 Crop and mat your photos then glue each to the page, as desired.

3 Hand-write or computer journal your story on white, then mat it on pink, leaving a ⅛" border. Cut a 4"x1⅞" rectangle of pink gingham and mat it on white, with a 1⁄16" border. Glue the journaling piece centered on the pink gingham, then glue it to the page. Punch hearts from the gingham and glue them as if spilling from the umbrella.

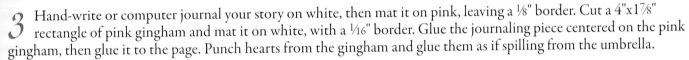

The Honeymoon by LeNae Gerig

Paper Pizazz® 12"x12" clouds paper
Paper Pizazz® 12"x12" sandstone paper
Paper Pizazz® 12"x12" palm leaves paper
blue paper
metallic black pen
alphabet template
straight-edged scissors
ruler and pencil
glue stick

1 Cut along the outer lines of some palm leaves about 4" from the bottom edge, as shown. Glue this portion along the lower edge of the clouds paper.

2 Hand-write or use a computer and printer to journal on white paper, then mat it on blue, leaving a ⅛" border. Crop and mat three photos, then glue the photos and journaling to the page as shown.

3 Use the template and the black pen to trace the letters of the destination; cut and glue them overlapping the photos.

Invitations, Announcements & More

Key Things to Keep in Mind:

The Wedding Colors: The color scheme you've chosen for your wedding can be reflected in your album and scrapbook pages. Use them in your matting and background choices when creating the album pages.

Carrying a Camera: Get used to carrying a camera around with you everywhere; or stock up on disposable cameras and keep one in your car, at work, at your friend's house. You'll always be prepared when the best photographic moments arrive.

When to Put it All Together: Create your album pages as each event takes place, or you may want to do it all after the honeymoon. Either way, keep those photos organized by writing dates, times, places and people within each set to avoid loosing the details of each memory.

Key Events to Photograph:

The Engagement: A formal photograph can be taken, either professionally or by a friend or family member to commemorate the event. Another suggestion is to take photos of the ring in the box and where the proposal was made. Make photocopies of your newspaper engagement announcement, as newsprint contains lignin, which will fade in time and can damage photos. Also, keepsakes can be added to albums, such as trinkets, cards or dried petals of your first bouquet from your fiancé.

Choosing the Wedding Attire: This is a great time to photograph the bride trying on dresses and the groom being fit for his tuxedo. Don't forget your bridal party in these photos, either. Some great candid shots can be captured!

The Bridal Shower: Photos of the activities and the opening of the gifts are natural shots to include. A group photo of all the guests with the bride in the center is a terrific addition to the album, as is a written list of the guests and gifts given.

Rehearsal and Dinner: Have various people photograph the rehearsal and dinner to obtain different viewpoints. A copy of the dinner menu is a perfect momento of the event.

The Morning of the Wedding: Capturing the full day on film is important. Start with the bride waking up, getting her hair done and those special moments before the ceremony. This is a great job for the your maid of honor and the groom's best man, even if you also have a professional photographer at the wedding.

The Wedding Ceremony: Consider handing out some disposal cameras to a select group of guests to photograph the ceremony from different vantage points. You'll be amazed at the different looks achieved and you'll enjoy scrapbooking the photographs.

The Reception: Get your wedding party to help photograph the reception, the tossing of the bouquet and the cutting of the cake, as well as shots of your guests.

Opening the Gifts: This is usually one of the last events of the wedding and a great time to photograph the gifts and guests. Also, keep a detailed copy of the gifts and guests to add as a momento to your scrapbook pages.

The Honeymoon: No matter where you spend your honeymoon, using fun theme papers can capture the memories forever. Keep a journal of what you did, where you went, special meals and unique excursions on the hotel stationery. Don't forget to photograph signs of the hotel and excursions you enjoyed. They're great for introducing sections within your album.

Faith, Hope & Love Album
by LeNae Gerig

9"x11" spiral bound photo album with a white or ivory cover

Paper Pizazz® soft tints 12"x12" yellow dots, soft tints 12"x12" yellow stripe

Paper Pizazz® white vellum

Paper Pizazz® solid ivory

Artsy Collage™ Embossed Words Paper Tags

2 gold metal wedding rings

12" of ⅝" wide sheer light yellow ribbon with iridescent edge

1 yard of ¼" wide sheer ivory ribbon

24" of yellow chenille fiber

hole punches: ⅛", ¼"

gold gel pen

computer and printer

glue stick

Helpful Hint
Use paper that compliments your wedding's colors or theme.

1 Remove the spiral binding from the album by simply pulling the round wire away from the album holes. Remove the cover and set the pages aside. Apply glue over the entire cover and smooth yellow dot paper over the glue. Place the dot paper face down on your work surface and trim the excess paper.

2 Place the corner of the album over the yellow stripe paper and cut a 2" wide triangle with the stripes running vertically. Glue a ¼" wide strip of ivory paper to the back of the long edge of the triangle. Trim the ivory paper to ⅛". Trim the ends even with the triangle. Repeat for a total of four triangles. Glue a triangle to each corner of the cover.

3 Turn the cover over and use the ¼" hole punch to punch through the holes covered by the paper. Print out a personalized title for the album on ivory paper. Trim the paper to fit your title with at least ¼" of space on each side of the text. Mat it on vellum with a ⅛" border. Mat it on yellow stripe paper with a ¼" border. Mat it on vellum again with a ⅛" border. Glue the matted title to the center of the cover. Draw a gold dot in each corner as shown with the pen.

4 Replace the cover onto the album. Cut the ¼" ribbon and the chenille fiber in half. Use one length of chenille to tie all of the ribbons and the rings together to the top spiral. Arrange the ribbons so the ends are uneven. Cut out the paper tags and punch a ⅛" hole in the top of each. Thread each onto a length of chenille and glue them to the cover as shown. Knot each ribbon end and trim the ends at an angle.

Covered Card Box
by LeNae Gerig

13"x13"x7½" round papier mâché box with lid
1¼ yards of 7½" wide white flat lace
4 yards of ⅝" wide white gimp braid
6 white pearl loop picks, each with 2" loops and wire stems
1½ yards of 1½" wide white sheer ribbon with gold edges
1½ yards of ⅝" wide gold sheer ribbon
1 green silk ivy bush, with five 3"-5" sprigs of 1"-3" leaves
1 stem of white silk amaryllis, with two 5" wide blossoms, one 4" bud and eight 5" leaves
1 stem of yellow silk oncidium orchids, with many 1¼" wide blossoms
1 stem of ivory silk roses, with three 2½" wide blossoms and many leaves
white acrylic spray paint
26-gauge wire, wire cutters
tacky craft glue, 1" wide paintbrush
X-acto® knife, cutting surface
low temperature glue gun, glue sticks

Helpful Hint
Place the card box on the gift table. It is also help-ful to place a nicely lettered card with the word "CARDS" resting next to the box.

1 Box—place the lid upside down on a cutting surface. Use the X-acto® knife to cut a ¾"x6" slot 3" from the lid edge. With the lid right side up and the box upside down, spray paint both pieces evenly; let dry thoroughly. **Lace**—use a 1" wide brush to apply tacky glue to the box sides. Starting with one end of the lace, adhere it evenly around the box.

2 Gimp braid—cut three 41" strips. Glue one braid around the lower edge of the box. Glue one braid along the top and bot-tom edge of the lid. Glue the remaining braid around the slot on the lid; trim any excess braid.

3 Use the 1½" wide ribbon to make a puffy bow (see page 9) with four 3" loops and 9" tails. Glue it to the lid as shown. Use the ⅝" wide ribbon to make a puffy bow with a center loop, six 3" loops and no tails. Glue this bow to the center of the other bow.

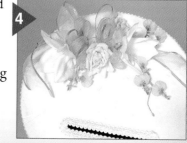

4 Cut all the roses with 1½" stems. Glue one to the bow center and two behind the bows, one angled left and one angled right. Cut each amaryllis stem to ½". Glue one under each side of the bows, extending outward. Cut the oncidium orchid sprigs from the stem and glue one on each side of each amaryllis. Cut the rose and amaryllis leaves with 1" stems and glue them evenly spaced extending outward from under the blossoms and bows. Cut the pearl loop stems to 1". Glue them evenly spaced among the blossoms as shown in the large photo.

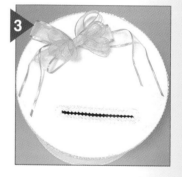

Mini Keepsake Album by LeNae Gerig

Paper Pizazz® yellow/green/lavender stripes, purple leaf sprigs, green with white dots papers
Paper Pizazz® 12"x12" lavender paper
Paper Pizazz® purple paper
two 3⅜" squares of posterboard
18" of ⅛" wide lavender satin ribbon
straight-edged scissors
black pen
tracing paper, transfer paper
ruler, pencil, glue stick

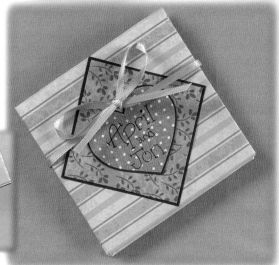

accordian fold inside

1   Cut two 4" squares from the stripes paper; glue a posterboard square centered on the back of each paper square. Fold each corner in diagonally and glue; fold in the sides and glue in place.

2   Cut two 3"x12" strips of lavender paper. Accordian fold each strip every 3". Glue the first panel on one strip to the end panel on the second strip, making a six-panel accordian.

3   Glue the accordian end panel to the inside of the covered posterboard and glue the opposite end panel to the inside of the other covered posterboard. Transfer the heart pattern to the dotted paper; cut it out and mat it on dark purple, leaving a ¹⁄₁₆" border. Cut out a 2⅛" square from the purple sprigs paper; mat it on dark purple, leaving a ¹⁄₁₆" border. Glue the heart centered to the square; glue the square centered as a diamond on the book front. Use the black pen to write a note of thanks or enclose some photos. Wrap the closed book with ribbon and tie a shoestring bow (see page 9) with 1½" loops and tails.

Mini "Thank You" Album by LeNae Gerig

Paper Pizazz® diagonal ribbons paper
white, ivory papers
two 4" squares of posterboard
24" of ⅜" wide sheer white ribbon with satin edges
1¼" wide gold heart charm with arrow
gold, black pens
straight-edged scissors
ruler, pencil, glue stick
stapler, staples
photos

1   Cut a 4½"x9" rectangle from diagonal ribbons paper; place it face down and glue a posterboard square ½" from each end, leaving a ¼" open in the center. Fold in each corner, then fold in the sides and ends, gluing them in place.

2   Cut three 7⅞"x3½" rectangles from the ivory paper. Glue one rectangle centered on the inside cover. Place the other two directly over the first ivory sheet and staple twice through all the layers along the center fold.

3   Wrap the ribbon through the book center and tie it in a shoestring bow (see page 9) on the front. Cut a 1¾" square of ivory; mat it on white, leaving a ¹⁄₁₆" border. With the gold pen, write "Love" and "Thank You" along the border. Glue the the square, angled and centered on the book front, then glue the charm in the center. Cut the photos, mat each, and glue them on the pages, then write the information near each.

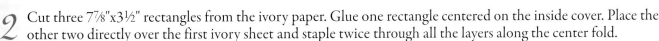

Bridal Headpieces

Crowns and caps, headbands and hats—so many choices when considering what headpiece is perfect for you! We may not eliminate choices, but we can help you narrow them a bit. First, decide how you'd like to wear your hair; once you know that, you can narrow your choices. Next, consider the type of ceremony you're planning—formal or informal. Both of these decisions will help determine the headpiece style.

Making your own headpiece is an excellent opportunity for saving money. A headpiece costing hundreds of dollars in a bridal shop can easily be created at a fraction of that price. The materials can be found in your local craft store—even finished veils that you attach to the headpiece—which allows you to create exactly what you want. You can also decide if you want the veil detachable for the reception celebration, which is especially convenient when wearing a long veil.

Match your dress by using ribbons and accents that coordinate with it; add pastel flowers to your headpiece if you want a touch of color; or mix ivory and white flowers together to provide depth to the headpiece and allow the flowers to show clearly. Making your own headpiece doesn't eliminate all those choices mentioned before, but it does allow you to have your perfect headpiece!

Bridal Headpieces

The headpiece or veil is the crowning touch for a bride and complements the theme of her wedding. The color scheme, array of floral treatments, time of day and site of the wedding all play important roles in the decision-making process. As an example, a long veil does not work well for outdoor weddings, because it may drag on the ground. In that case, a short fingertip-length veil or a headpiece with a detachable veil would work perfectly.

Veils

Pre-gathered veils with loops: Some veils come pre-gathered with small elastic loops sewn along the gathered area. The loops make it easy to attach the veil to hair combs.

Ready-to-gather veils: Some veils come with clear monofilament inserted along the upper edge. It is extremely secure and easy to gather the veil by pulling and pushing the fabric to the desired width.

pre-gathered veil with loops

ready-to-gather veil

Gathering tulle with a needle & thread: Knot one end of the thread and secure at one corner of the tulle. Begin sewing a running stitch ¼" from the top edge of the tulle and pull to gather the tulle to the desired width; secure with a knot at the opposite end.

gathering tulle with needle & thread
(red thread was used here for contrast)

Veil Edgings

No Edge: Tulle may be purchased in widths of 54" or 108" without any edging embellishment. Because tulle doesn't fray easily, you can leave the edges plain or you can enhance the edges with ribbon, beading or other materials.

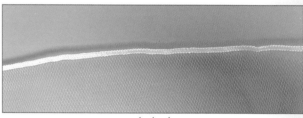

corded edge

Corded Edges: Most veils with edging are pre-made and require little work to achieve the desired look. A corded edge on a veil is a simple, yet elegant enhancement; these veils are readily available in most craft stores.

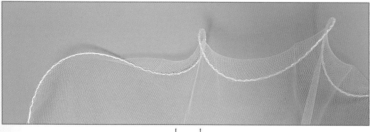

curly edge

Curly Edge: For a dramatic look, curly edges provide a whimsical dimension, with structured edges allowing the veil to stand slightly away from the body. The curled edges can be found on the veil ends as well as in the pouffs and are available in most craft stores.

pearl edge

Pearl Edge: This edging is classically sophisticated and is best worn with gowns of classic lines using few embellishments to showcase the bride.

Helpful Hint

Veil lengths should complement the formality of your wedding. The more formal the ceremony, the longer the veil. Shoulder and elbow lengths work well with informal and outdoor settings, while chapel and cathedral lengths should only be used indoors in formal settings.

How to Attach a Veil to a Headpiece:

Using Glue: Place the headpiece on a flat surface, with the area you will be gluing face up. Apply a fine line of glue where you will be attaching the gathered area of the veil. Gently press the gathers to the glue until set in place.

Attaching a veil with loops: If your veil comes with pre-sewn loops, glue the veil to the headpiece so a comb may be attached by weaving the teeth of the comb through the loops.

Sewing a hair comb to a veil: Use a sewing needle and matching thread to attach the comb to the gathered edge of the tulle. Stitch through the tulle and wrap the thread around the right and left ends of the comb several times to secure; knot each end between the comb and gathers.

Gluing pearls & rhinestones: Separate the veil layers and place wax paper under the area where you plan to glue a pearl or rhinestone—this will prevent the glue from adhering the tulle to your work surface. Use a small dot of fabric glue to attach the pearl or rhinestone to the tulle. Repeat to add more pearls or rhinestones. If the veil will be worn over your face, determine whether you want the pearls on the outside when the veil covers your face or when it's turned back over your head.

Using Velcro®: Use non-adhesive Velcro® for the veil. The adhesive type Velcro® can stick to your hair and is difficult to remove. Glue the hook piece of Velcro® to the underside of the headpiece and the loop piece to the gathered edge of the veil. This provides a great option for removing the veil during the reception, while still wearing the headpiece.

gluing a hair comb to the veil

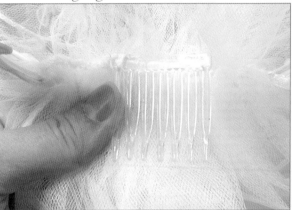
sewing a hair comb to the veil

gluing a pearl to the veil

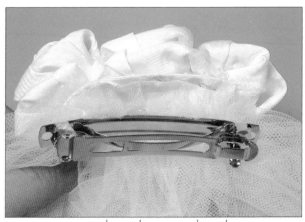
attaching a barrett to the veil

using Velcro® with the veil

Bridal Headpieces

Designer Tip

We've used shoulder lengths of tulle for these stunning, yet simple-to-make headpieces. If you'd like a longer veil, simply purchase 108" wide tulle in longer lengths.

Pearl Studded Headpiece

by LeNae Gerig

7"x2¼" pearl studded ivory headpiece with comb
30"x30" two-tiered ivory veil with corded edges
twenty-four 4mm ivory pearls
fabric glue
low temperature glue gun, glue sticks
wax paper

1 Gather the veil to 6½"; use the glue gun to adhere the gathered portion between the comb and headpiece.

2 Separate the veil layers. Place wax paper between the layers. Use the fabric glue to adhere the pearls to the top layer of the veil; let dry and remove the wax paper.

Floral Barrette

by LeNae Gerig

3" long metal barrette
two 7" long sheer white and silk flower sprays, each with six 2" wide blossoms and two 2" long pearl stems
five 1" wide white satin rose buds
four 1½" wide sheer white ribbon roses
one 3" wide sheer white ribbon rose
white floral tape
wire cutter
low temperature glue gun, glue sticks

1 Cut the sprays to 5" long and place one on the left and one on the right of the clip so the flowers span 9". Overlap the stems in the center of the barrette and secure them with floral tape. Bend each outer end of the sprays so they curve downward. Cut the 3" rose from the stem and glue it over where the spray stems meet.

2 Cut the satin and sheer rose stems to ½" long. Pull the spray blossoms up and out from the stems and glue two 1½" sheer roses on each side of the 3" sheer rose, extending out. Glue two satin rose buds evenly spaced on the left side and three on the right.

Pearl & Rhinestone Flower Tiara
by LeNae Gerig

pearl & rhinestone flower tiara
38"x72" blunt edge white tulle veil with pearls and comb

back view

*S*imply bobby pin the veil at the base of the hairstyle or use the comb to attach the veil. For a "waterfall" effect, incorporate the veil into the hairstyle.

Floral Wreath with Veil & Pouff
by LeNae Gerig

2" wide white wire headband with white satin flowers, pearl accents and attached comb
17"x24" two-tiered white tulle veil with corded white pouff
low temperature glue gun, glue sticks

1 Wire the headband ends together to fit around the bride's head. Gather the veil to 4½" wide and glue the gathered portion to the back of the headband.

2 Separate the layers of the pouff to make them stand upright.

Helpful Hint
Pouffs add dimension to a wedding headpiece and are available ready-made in most craft and fabric stores. Some come without edging enhancements, while others feature corded or lace edgings.

Bridal Headpieces

Floral Wreath

by LeNae Gerig

38"x72" blunt edge white tulle veil with pearls and comb
2 stems of yellow silk roses, each with fourteen 2"-3" long stems of
  ¾"-1" wide blossoms, open buds and many
    1" long leaves
3 stems of white silk roses, each with fourteen 2"-3" long stems of
  ¾"-1" wide blossoms, open buds and many 1" long leaves
4 daisy stems, each with five 3" long stems each with one ⅝" wide
  blossom and one 6" long stem with many ⅝" wide blossoms
1 yard of white 3mm fused pearls
green floral tape
24-gauge paddle wire
bobby pins
measuring tape
low temperature glue gun, glue sticks

1 Measure the circumference around the styled "up do." Add 2" to the measurement for the wire for the wreath. Wrap the wire with floral tape and bend it into a round shape. Follow step 2 on page 86 for the Flower Girl Head Wreath to secure the flowers to the wire, leaving 1" of wire at each end.

2 Glue one end of the pearls to one end of the flowers. Wrap them around the flowers and glue at the opposite end. Trim any excess. Wrap the wreath around the hair style and twist the wire ends together to secure. Use bobby pins to secure the garland to her hair. Insert the veil under the wreath.

Rhinestone Headpiece & Veil

by LeNae Gerig

7"x1½" white satin curved bar headpiece with pearls &
  rhinestones and attached to a comb
30"x30" two-tiered white tulle veil with corded edges
fifteen 2mm clear rhinestones
fabric glue
low temperature glue gun, glue sticks
wax paper

1 Slightly separate the comb from the headpiece. Gather the veil (if necessary) and use the glue gun to adhere the gathered edge between the comb and headpiece.

2 Separate the veil layers and place wax paper between them. Use fabric glue to adhere the rhinestones to the top layer of the veil; let dry and remove the wax paper.

Floral Hair Clip
by LeNae Gerig

two 2" wide ivory ribbon poinsettias with pearl centers
four ¾" wide ivory ribbon roses with green leaves
five ⅜" wide ivory ribbon roses with green leaves
three 1¼" wide ivory ribbon carnations
6" square of ivory satin fabric
3"x4" rectangle of cardboard
3" wide hair clip
tracing paper, transfer paper
pencil
low temperature glue gun, glue sticks

1 Trace each of the ovals and transfer them to the cardboard; cut the ovals out. Place the large oval on a 4½"x3" rectangle of fabric; fold the fabric to the back of the oval and glue the edges in place. Repeat to cover the small oval. Glue the ovals together back-to-back, with the smaller oval centered on the larger one.

2 Glue the flowers to the front of the large oval, arranged as shown, then glue the hair clip to the back.

Designer Tip
This enchanting hair clip can also be made for your bridesmaids. Simply choose the ribbon flower colors to coordinate with the color of their dresses.

Ribbon Rose Veil
by LeNae Gerig

3" wide clear hair comb
two 2" wide white satin ribbon roses
three 2" wide white sheer ribbon roses
20" of ⅝" wide white satin ribbon
2 yards of 54" wide white tulle
sewing needle, white thread
low temperature glue gun, glue sticks

1 Gather one short side of the tulle; glue it to the top edge of the hair comb. Center and glue an 8" length of satin ribbon to cover the raw edge of the tulle, wrapping the ends to the underside of the comb.

2 Glue the roses to the satin ribbon area on the comb, alternating the rose styles and angling them over the edge. Use the remaining ribbon to make a Dior bow (see page 9) with 2" loops. Glue it to cover the "stem" ends of the ribbon roses.

Bridal Headpieces

Pearl Wrapped Headband
by LeNae Gerig

white satin covered headband
8½ yards of 3mm white fused pearls
38"x72" blunt edge white tulle veil with pearls
6" of ⅜" wide white sew-on Velcro® (optional)
white thread, needle
tacky craft glue
low temperature glue gun, glue sticks

1 Hot glue one end of the pearl length to the inside bottom of one side of the headband. Place a 1" line of tacky glue on the center of the outside of the headband. Wrap the pearls around the headband, keeping the strands close together and adding glue as you go. Hot glue the end of the pearls to the inside of the headband.

2 Gather the veil to 6" wide and sew the loop half (fuzzy) of the Velcro® to the gather. Glue the hook half (prickly) to the back half of the underside of the headband. Press the pieces together to attach the veil.

Designer Tip

After the ceremony, simply detach the veil piece and just wear the headband for the reception festivities. If you wish to make the veil a permanent part of the headpiece, glue it directly to the headband.

Bow Hair Clip
by LeNae Gerig

5½"x2¼" white satin double bow with hair clip
16" length of 24"x50" two-tiered white veil with corded edges
low temperature glue gun, glue sticks

Gather the pre-gathered edge of the veil to 2½" wide. Tuck and glue this portion between the clip and bow.

Designer Tip

You can easily make this bow in other colors: Cut a 3", 10" and 12" lengths of the desired ribbon. Form the 12" length into a circle and pinch the center to make the bow shape. Repeat with the 10" length and center it over the first bow. Fold the 3" length into thirds and wrap it around the center of the two bows. Glue the bows over a 3" long hair clip.

Ivory Fabric Rose Headpiece
by LeNae Gerig

2 yards of 54" wide ivory tulle
ivory satin moiré fabric: two 2"x17" rectangles, one 3"x17" rectangle and a 5" square
twenty-four 4mm white pearls
3" long hair clip
9" length of 26-gauge white cloth-covered wire
sewing machine, ivory thread
sewing needle
tracing paper, transfer paper
3"x1½" rectangle of cardboard
fabric glue
wax paper
low temperature glue gun, glue sticks

1 Fold the 3"x17" rectangle of moiré fabric in half down the long side; with a sewing machine, sew a running stitch ¼" from the long edge, forming a tube. Turn the tube right side out, then repeat the process to make two more tubes.

2 Cut the cloth-covered wire into 3" lengths. Follow the directions below to make a 2½" wide rose from the 3"x17" fabric tube; secure the rose with the wire. Repeat the process with each of the two remaining tubes to make 1½" wide ribbon roses.

3 Transfer the oval pattern onto the cardboard; cut it out. Cut a 3"x4" rectangle from the square of moiré. Cover the cardboard with fabric, gluing the edges at the back. Cut an oval from the remaining piece of fabric and glue it to the back of the fabric-covered oval.

4 Glue the larger ribbon rose centered on the oval, with a small rose on each side. Cut the tulle into two 36"x54" pieces. With one placed directly on top of the other, use needle and thread to gather the 36" long edges ½" from the top to 2½" wide and secure. Glue the gathered end to the back of the fabric-covered oval, then glue the oval to the hair clip top.

5 Spread just the top tulle layer of the veil on a flat surface. Place the wax paper underneath the tulle, place a dot of fabric glue and press a pearl into the glue dot. Repeat to glue the remaining pearls evenly spaced over the top layer of the veil. Let dry and remove the wax paper.

How to Make a Fabric Rose:

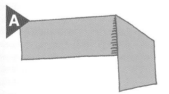

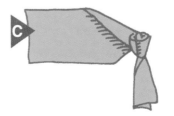

A. Fold the right end down diagonally.

B. Tightly roll the strip two turns to the left, then fold the left end back and down. Holding the tail firmly, roll another half turn to the left.

C. Fold the left end so the bottom edge is now on top. Continue to roll and fold until there is only a 1" tail remaining on the left.

D. Bring the tails together and wrap with wire to secure.

Bridal Headpieces

Pearl & Rose Headband
by LeNae Gerig

16" headband made with 6mm & 3mm ivory pearl beads

30"x30" two-tiered ivory tulle veil with corded edges

2" wide ivory floral spray with a 1½" wide tulle rose, ten 1½" wide silk/pearl/tulle flower blossoms and six 2" long ivory leaves

1 stem of ivory silk roses, with six 1" wide ivory open blossoms

twenty 4mm ivory pearls

fabric glue

low temperature glue gun, glue sticks

wax paper

Designer Tip

Have your hairdresser or attendant attach the wreath to your hair with bobby pins so it stays beautifully in place.

1 Form the headband into a circle to fit comfortably on the bride's head. Secure it by twisting the ends together.

2 Gather the veil to 6" wide; glue the gathered edge to the wired section of the headband.

3 Glue the floral spray over the gathered ends of the veil and allow it to dry thoroughly.

4 Cut each open rose stem to 1½" long. Glue a rose to each side of the center rose in the spray. Glue two more roses among the flowers on each side of the first rose. Attach a hair comb, if necessary. Place wax paper between the veil layers; use the fabric glue to adhere the pearls to the veil. Let dry.

Floral Headband with Veil
by LeNae Gerig

1¼" wide white padded satin headband
30"x30" two-tiered white tulle veil with
   corded edges
1 white bridal floral spray with three 1½" wide
   silk magnolias with pearl centers, three 3" long
   pearl sprays and 3 leaves
1 white bridal floral spray with three 2" wide silk
   and tulle hibiscus blossoms and 1 leaf
1 white satin rose spray with three 1½" wide blossoms with pearl centers and 3 leaves
1 white satin bridal rosebud spray with five 1½"
   wide buds
1 white bridal floral spray with six 1½" wide silk/
   tulle starflowers with pearl centers, six 3" long
   pearl sprays and 6 leaves
1 cluster of white satin ribbon flowers with four 1"
   wide flowers with pearl centers and 4 leaves
low temperature glue gun, glue sticks

1 Cut each flower blossom stem to ¼" long. Cut the leaves and pearl sprays from the stems. The flowers are glued to the headband center area, leaving 2" on each end uncovered. Begin with the magnolia blossoms: glue one left of the center top with one 2" away on each side. Glue the hibiscus blossoms next: one right of center, angled back, and the others 2" away on each side.

2 Glue a 1½" rose next to each hibiscus, all angled toward the back. Glue all the remaining blossoms and leaves evenly spaced among the roses, hibiscus and magnolias, covering the headband to within 2" of each end. Glue the leaves to extend from under the blossoms and curve naturally outward. Glue the pearl sprays angled downwards on each end.

3 Gather the veil to 6" wide if necessary and, beginning at the center of the headband, glue the gathered edge of the veil to the inner back edge of the headband. As an option, a comb may be sewn in place, depending on the hair style.

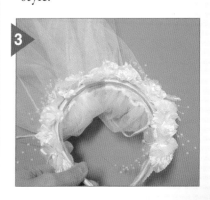

The Tiara

The tiara creates a royal atmosphere fit for a princess. It works best with "Cinderella" and fairy tale themed weddings. Most tiaras come with clear glass rhinestones and fit directly on top of the head. Be sure to look for one which will allow a veil to be attached to cascade down the back. Whether the bride's hair is styled high on the head or down as shown here, this headpiece is striking.

Rhinestone Tiara with Veil

by LeNae Gerig

tiara with clear glass rhinestones
30"x30" white tulle veil
sewing needle, white thread
bobby pins or hair comb

Place the tiara on top of the bride's head. Gather the veil edge and use bobby pins or a haircomb to insert into the hair at the back of the head.

Helpful Hint

Add more sparkle to your headpiece by gluing single rhinestones evenly spaced on the top of the tulle veil.

Headpiece Storage Box
by LeNae Gerig

10"x10"x5" round papier mâché box
pieces of ivory woven cotton fabric: 5"x30", 1"x30", 11" square
1 yard of 1½" wide ivory satin moiré ribbon with wired edges
2½ yards of ⅜" wide white satin braid
twenty-eight 8mm white flat-back round pearls
six 1¼" long white pearl loop leaves on white wire stems
twelve ½" wide white clay rosebuds on green wire stems
six ¾" wide white clay rose blossoms, each with a 1" leaf on green wire stems
twelve 1" wide ivory silk carnations with pearl centers
1 stem of green silk ivy with fourteen 1"-2" wide leaves
ivory acrylic paint, ½" wide flat paintbrush
26-gauge wire, wire cutters
low temperature glue gun, glue sticks
tacky craft glue, pencil and scissors

1 Paint the box (not the lid) ivory and let dry. Glue the 5" wide fabric around the box side, making sure the top and bottom edges are securely

adhered, with the end folded under. Place the 11" square of fabric face down. Place the box lid centered, top side down, on the fabric and trace around the lid. Cut out the circle and glue it on the lid, then glue the 1" strip to the outer edge of the lid.

2 Cut the braid into three 10" lengths. Glue one along the bottom edge of the box, covering the raw edge of the fabric. Glue one braid along the bottom edge of the lid and one along the top edge.

3 Use the ribbon to make a puffy bow (see page 9) with a center loop, six 2½" loops and no tails; secure the bow with the wire, cutting off any excess. Glue the

bow at the edge of the lid near the side seam. Cut the stems of the clay rosebuds and blossoms and silk carnations to 1½". Glue the flowers evenly spaced among the bow loops.

4 Cut the sprigs from the ivy vine. Glue the leaves extending outward from under the bow side loops, and a few extending from the center loop. Cut the

pearl leaf stems to 1½", then glue them evenly spaced among the flowers and leaves. Use the tacky glue to adhere seven half pearls to the lid sides and the remaining half pearls staggered in two rows evenly spaced around the box base.

Special Accessories

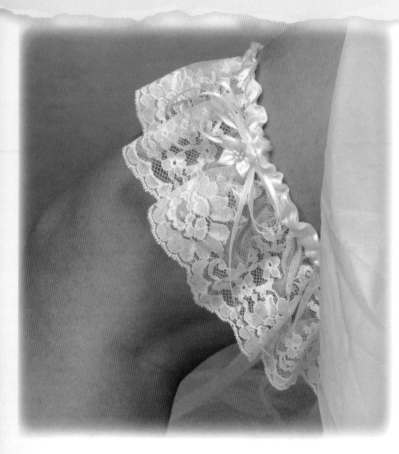

Easy Garter
by LeNae Gerig

3¾" wide white lace (length depends on thigh measurement)
⅝" wide white satin ribbon (length depends on thigh measurement)
30" length of ⅛" wide white satin ribbon
¼" wide white elastic (length depends on thigh measurement)
1" wide white satin flower with pearl center
sewing machine, white thread
sewing needle
straight pins
safety pin or bobkin
fabric glue
measuring tape

Designer Tip
Since this garter is so easy to make, consider making two—one to keep and another for the groom to toss.

1 Measure the bride's thigh. For the elastic: subtract 3" from the thigh measurement. For the lace and ⅝" wide ribbon: double the measurement.

2 **Lace**—pin the ⅝" ribbon along the top edge of the lace; use the sewing machine to stitch ⅛" from the top and bottom edges of the ribbon, forming a tube for the elastic.

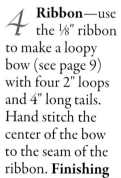

Red thread was used here for clarity.

3 **Elastic**—attach the safety pin to one end of the elastic and thread it through the tube, making sure the free end doesn't slip inside the tube. Double stitch through all the layers on each end to secure the elastic. Position the raw ends of the lace right sides together and stitch.

4 **Ribbon**—use the ⅛" ribbon to make a loopy bow (see page 9) with four 2" loops and 4" long tails. Hand stitch the center of the bow to the seam of the ribbon. **Finishing touch:** use fabric glue to adhere the flower to the center of the bow.

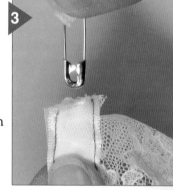

40

Flower Girl Rose Ball
by LeNae Gerig

2" wide Styrofoam® ball
seven 1¼" wide pink paper roses
nine 1¼" wide white paper roses
thirteen ¾" wide pink paper rosebuds, each with a 1" leaf
thirteen ¾" wide white paper rosebuds, each with a 1" leaf
1 yard of 1" wide pink sheer organza ribbon
26-gauge wire, wire cutters
low temperature glue gun, glue sticks

1 **Roses**—cut each blossom and bud stem to ½". Glue the wider pink roses evenly around the ball; then repeat with the wider white roses. Fill in the empty spaces by gluing the smaller pink and white roses to the ball.

2 **Ribbon**—cut it into three 12" lengths. Wrap the end of one strip with wire to make a loop. Twist the wire several times, leaving ½" end of wire. Glue the wire end to the ball.

3 **Finishing touch:** fold the two remaining ribbon strips in 4"-8" lengths, then wrap wire around the folds; twist several times, leaving ½" wire end. Glue the wire end to the center bottom of the ball.

Flower Girl Slippers
by LeNae Gerig

1 pair of child's white leather ballet slippers
24" of ⅛" wide pink satin ribbon
two 1¼" wide pink tulle flowers, each with a ¼" wide pink ribbon rose center
26-gauge wire, wire cutters
low temperature glue gun, glue sticks

Cut the ribbon in half. Use each length to make a loopy bow (see page 9) with four 1" loops. Wrap wire around the center of each bow and twist twice. Cut the wire ends. Glue a bow to the front edge of each slipper as shown, then glue a flower to the center of each bow.

Designer Tip
Choose ribbons and flowers to match your wedding theme.

Wedding Favors

Wedding celebrations are meant to be shared and remembered. Traditionally, small momentos or favors are given to friends and relatives to commemorate the celebration. Your wedding day will be memorable for everyone, especially when your favors are as pretty as those included here.

Making your own favors provides another opportunity for saving on expenses. Easy and quick to assemble, these favors are perfect for any wedding—and because we've listed the components, you can match your wedding colors, creating favors that coordinate perfectly. To personalize a favor, attach a decorative tag or strip of paper to it which includes the names of the bride and groom, the date and perhaps a short message. Inside each favor, include treats you and your fiancé especially like or a non-edible keepsake, such as a poem that conveys your feelings and wishes.

The materials used in creating these favors are found in most craft stores, making it very convenient to pull all the pieces together. To make the assembly process more fun, include it as part of the wedding festivities by inviting your attendants together to make the favors. Whether your wedding is a simple affair or a gala event, here you'll find the perfect favors to present to your guests with pride. And you'll feel especially good knowing you saved money while creating each one.

Wedding Favors

Rose Petal Favor

by LeNae Gerig

9" wide circle of pink tulle
9" of ⅛" wide pink satin ribbon
¾" wide iridescent pink flower
⅛ cup of dried rose petals
low temperature glue gun, glue sticks

1 Remove the petals from a fresh rose in full bloom; discarding any petals with brown edges. Scatter the petals on a sheet of clean newspaper and place in a cool, dry location for one week.

2 Place the dried petals in the center of the tulle and gather the edges. Wrap the ribbon tightly around the gathered portion and tie in a shoestring bow (see page 9) with two 1" loops and two 1" tails. Glue the flower to the bow center.

Designer Tip

If you can't find enough fresh rose petals, consider silk rose petals. They look just like the real thing and are available in most craft stores.

Helpful Hint

Add more sparkle to these favors by choosing tulle with metallic specks. It's available in most craft stores.

Mint Candy Favor

by LeNae Gerig

two 9" wide circles of white tulle
9" of ⅜" wide white sheer ribbon with white satin edges
4 green mint candies

Stack the tulle circles together, then place the mints in the center of the tulle. Gather the tulle edges around the candy and wrap the ribbon tightly around the gathered portion. Tie a shoestring bow (see page 9) with two 1" loops and two 1" tails.

Designer Tip

With mint candies available in most all colors, choose ones which complement your wedding theme.

Champagne Glass
by LeNae Gerig

2"x2" clear acrylic champagne glass
9" wide circle of white tulle with gold flecks
9" of ⅛" wide white satin ribbon
4 yellow mint candies

Place the mints inside the glass then position the circle centered over the top. Gather the edges around the glass stem and wrap the ribbon tightly around the gathered tulle. Tie the ribbon in a shoestring bow (see page 9) with two 1" loops and two 1" tails to secure the tulle.

Glass Slipper
by LeNae Gerig

4¼" long clear acrylic slipper
12" square of white tulle
5" of ½" wide lavender sheer ribbon with satin ribbon center
4 lavender Jordan almonds

Place the almonds in the slipper and place it centered on the tulle square. Gather the four corners together above the slipper. Wrap the ribbon tightly around the gathered tulle and knot to secure the gathered edges.

Swan Cup
by LeNae Gerig

4" clear acrylic swan cup
9" wide circle of pink tulle
six ¾" wide pink silk daisies
6" of ½" wide white sheer ribbon with satin ribbon center
5 pink Jordan almonds
low temperature glue gun, glue sticks

Place the almonds centered on the tulle and gather the edges together. Wrap the ribbon tightly around the gathered tulle and knot to secure the gathered edges. Glue five daisies to the swan's neck, as shown. Glue the remaining daisy to the bow center and place the almonds in the swan cup.

Wedding Favors

Keepsake Bags by LeNae Gerig

12" of ¼" wide ivory satin cord
   (for each bag)
sewing machine
straight pins
For the beige bag: two 3½"x7"
   rectangles of heavy weight beige
   tapestry fabric
beige thread
For the green bag: two 4½"x7"
   rectangles of green moiré fabric
green thread

1 Pin the right sides of the fabric pieces together. Sew ¼" from the edge along one long side; secure each end by backstitching several times.

2 Remove the pins and open the fabric; fold 1" from the front to the back along the top edge and sew a running stitch to secure. Place the right sides together, again; sew the bottom and other side together. Turn the bag right side out and fill it with a surprise. Tie the cord around the neck of the bag in a knot, then knot each cord end.

Designer Tip
These bags take just minutes to make. And, it's a great way to use the remnants from the bridesmaids' dresses.

White Fringed Bag

by LeNae Gerig

3"x3½" white sheer organza bag with ribbon drawstring
7" of 1½" wide clear beaded fringe with white satin rib-
   bon band
five 4mm clear rhinestones
3" square of wax paper
7 white Jordan almonds
fabric glue

1 Insert wax paper inside the bag to prevent glue from soaking through to the other side. Beginning at the back center, glue the satin band of the fringe along the bottom edge of the bag; let dry. Glue rhinestones to the front of the bag evenly spaced, as shown; let dry.

2 Remove the wax paper and fill the bag with the candy; pull the drawstring closed to secure.

Designer Tip

If you want a little color in the bag, simply add colored mints.

Shopping Bag

by LeNae Gerig

2½"x3" white papier mâché shopping bag with 2½" tall
   handles
10" of 1½" wide pink with white dots wire edge ribbon
10" of ¾" wide white satin ribbon
10" of ⅛" wide pink with white dots satin ribbon
two 9" circles of pink tulle
two silver metal wedding rings
candy or a small gift
low temperature glue gun, glue sticks

1 Glue one end of the 1½" ribbon to the center of one short side of the bag. Wrap the ribbon around the sides of the bag, gluing as you wrap. Fold the raw end under and glue it over the first end.

2 Hold the remaining ribbons together and tie them around the left front handle into a shoestring bow (see page 9) with 1" loops and 2" tails. Trim the ends at an angle. Glue the rings under the bows as shown. Wrap the candy or gift in the tulle and place it inside.

Wedding Favors

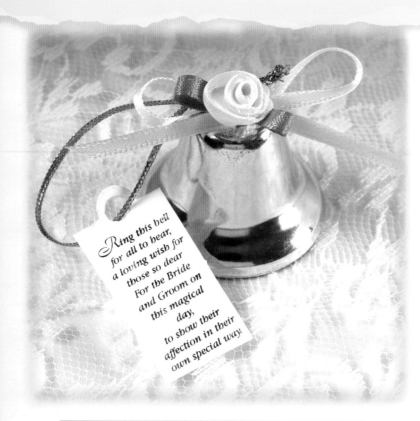

Gold Bell with Special Message Tag
by LeNae Gerig

*1⅜"x1⅜" gold liberty bell with attached
    message tag*
9" of ⅛" wide ivory satin ribbon
*⅜" wide ivory ribbon rose with two green satin
    ribbon leaves*
low temperature glue gun, glue sticks

Use the ribbon to make a shoestring bow (see
page 9) with two 1" loops and two 1¼" tails.
Glue it centered to the top of the bell with the
rose glued to the bow center.

Designer Tip

*We've used a pre-printed message tag
for this delightful bell. You can also
make your own special message tag
with the bride and groom's name and
wedding date to commemorate the
occasion.*

Designer Tip

*Your guests can use these bell favors as great
Christmas decorations after the wedding.*

Gold Bell with Burgundy Flower
by LeNae Gerig

1⅜"x1⅜" gold liberty bell
14" of ⅛" wide burgundy satin ribbon
¾" wide burgundy cloth flower with 1" leaf
low temperature glue gun, glue sticks

1 Cut the ribbon in half; hold the pieces
together and thread them through the bell
loop; tie them into a shoestring bow (see page
9) with four ¾" loops and four 2" tails. Glue the
flower to the bow center.

Helpful Hint

*Favors are a special gift for your guests at the
wedding ceremony and the reception. Hand
these charming bells to your guests before the
wedding, so they can use them to "ring" in your
union.*

Votive Candle

by LeNae Gerig

9" wide circle of white tulle with gold flecks
9" of ⅛" wide burgundy satin ribbon
1" wide burgundy tulle flower with ribbon rose center
1½" tall green votive candle
low temperature glue gun, glue sticks

Place the candle centered on the tulle circle. Gather the edges over the top of the candle and twist once. Wrap the ribbon tightly around the gathered section and tie in a shoestring bow (see page 9) with two 1" loops and two 1½" tails. Glue the flower to the bow center.

Designer Tip

There are a variety of scented candles available, so choose your favorite scents. Also, try mixing and matching colors for a variety of looks.

Candy Votive

by LeNae Gerig

2¼"x1⅞" clear glass votive cup
12" square of white tulle
12" of ⅜" wide white sheer ribbon with satin edges
two 1¼" wide white plastic doves
¾" wide white silk flower
8-10 Jordan almonds
low temperature glue gun, glue sticks

1 Wash the votive cup and let it dry thoroughly; then fill it with the almonds. Place the votive centered on the tulle square; gather the four corners together and twist once. Wrap the ribbon tightly around the gathered section and tie in a shoestring bow (see page 9) with two 1" loops and two 1½" tails. Glue the doves to the bow center, facing each other, then glue the flower centered below the doves.

Vellum Cone
by LeNae Gerig

7" square of Paper Pizazz® vellum dots paper
9" of ⅛" wide pink satin ribbon
6-8 fresh or silk rose petals
glue stick
pencil

1 Place the vellum paper over the circle pattern (see page 143) and lightly trace around the outline. Cut the circle out and roll the bottom edge into a cone shape. Place a dab of glue between the overlap.

2 Wrap the ribbon around the cone as shown and tie it in a shoestring bow (see page 9) with two 1" loops and two 1" tails. Fill the cone with the petals. At the reception, have an attendent give a cone to each guest to toss the petals onto the newly married couple as they leave the reception.

Designer Tip

If you plan to make 25 or more of these favors, order the paper in 25 or 50-sheet packages. See page 143 for other alternatives to tracing the circle and pyramid box.

Rose Pyramid Box
by LeNae Gerig

8½"x11" sheet of Paper Pizazz® muted roses paper
9" of ⅛" wide pink satin ribbon
tracing paper, transfer paper
⅛" wide hole punch
tacky craft glue
pencil

1 Trace the pyramid pattern (see page 143) onto tracing paper; transfer the pattern onto the back of the roses paper. Cut out the pattern and use the hole punch to cut out the holes where indicated on the pattern.

2 Fold the pyramid along the dotted lines as shown on the pattern; use a small dot of glue on each side to secure. Fill the pyramid with candy or a small surprise. Thread the ribbon through the holes and tie into a shoestring bow (see page 9) to secure.

Pearl Accent Box
by LeNae Gerig

3"x3"x2" papier mâché box
20" of ⅝" wide ivory satin picot ribbon
ivory round flat-backed pearls: 15mm,
*   six 8mm*
white acrylic paint
acrylic sealer
½" wide flat paintbrush
tacky craft glue

1 Seal the box and lid and let dry. Paint the box and lid white; let both pieces dry thoroughly.

2 Place a surprise in the box and replace the lid. Place the box in the center of the ribbon; wrap the ribbon from each side to the top. Tie a shoestring bow (see page 9) centered on the lid with two 1½" loops and two 1½"tails. Glue the 15mm half pearl to the center of the bow. Glue the 8mm pearls evenly spaced around the lid side.

Seeds of Love
by LeNae Gerig

5" square of Paper Pizazz® lavender vellum paper
Paper Flair™ 2 Envelopes Template
1" wide ivory satin bow with pearl center
flower seeds
glue stick

1 Use the mini envelope template or the pattern on page 141 to trace the shape onto the vellum. Cut it out. Fold in each side, then fold the bottom upward; secure the edges with glue and let dry.

2 Fill the envelope with flower seeds; fold the top flap down and glue the edges to secure. Glue the bow centered on the top flap, as shown.

Designer Tip
This favor is perfect for spring weddings and a way for your guests to remember your special day by planting the seeds from the favor. Choose flower seeds suitable for your growing region.

Wedding Favors

Paper Box
by LeNae Gerig

Paper Pizazz® 8½"x11" diagonal ribbons paper
1 yard of ⅛" wide ivory satin ribbon
⅜" wide ivory ribbon rose with two green ribbon
  leaves
tracing paper, transfer paper
tacky craft glue
pencil

1 Trace the box pattern (see page 142) onto tracing paper, then transfer the pattern to the back of the ribbons paper. Cut out the box. Fold the box along the dotted lines as shown on the pattern; glue the sides to secure, but leave the lid free. Insert candy or a small surprise and fold in the lid.

2 Place the box upside down in the center of the ribbon and wrap as for a package. Tie a shoestring bow (see page 9) with two 1½" loops and two 2½" tail. Glue the rose to the bow center.

Designer Tip

If you plan to make 25 or more of the box favors, order the paper in 25 or 50 sheet packages. See page 142 for alternatives to tracing the pattern.

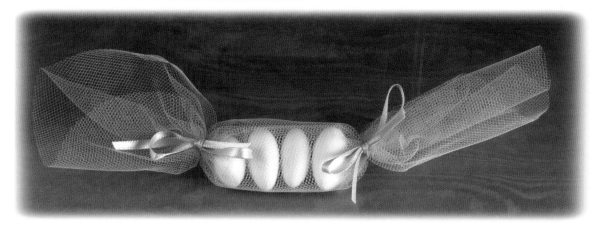

Candy Roll by LeNae Gerig

9" wide circle of lavender tulle
12" of ⅛" wide lavender satin ribbon
4 Jordan almonds
tacky craft glue

Place the candy centered on the tulle circle. Fold the circle in half over the candy and roll into a tube. Use a tiny dab of glue to secure the edge of the tulle tube. Cut the ribbon in half. Wrap one piece around each end of the tube, making a shoestring bow (see page 9) with two 1" loops and two 1" tails.

Take-Out Box
by LeNae Gerig

8½"x11" sheet of white cardstock
10" of 24-gauge plastic covered green craft wire
15"x2" strip of white tulle
three ¾" wide iridescent pink cloth flowers
three 1" wide silk ivy leaves
tracing paper, transfer paper
⅛" hole punch, pencil
tacky craft glue
low temperature glue gun, glue sticks

1 Trace the take-out box pattern (see page 141) onto tracing paper; transfer the pattern onto the back of the cardstock. Cut out the pattern and use the hole punch to cut out the holes where shown on the pattern. Fold the box along the dotted lines as shown on the pattern; glue the sides to secure, but leave the flaps free. Fill the box with candy or a small surprise and close the flaps.

2 Bend each end of the wire into a ½" hook (see pattern on page 141); insert the ends into the holes on the box sides. Glue the ivy leaves onto the box front as shown, glue the flowers centered on the leaves. Wrap the tulle around the handle center and tie it into a shoestring bow (see page 9) with two 2" loops and two 2½" tails.

Designer Tip
These adorable favors are perfect for the reception. Have one placed at the table for each guest or at a table near the entrance door.

Cherub Basket
by LeNae Gerig

2"x2½" white plastic basket with 1¾" tall handle
12" square of white tulle
1" iridescent white plastic cherub with string hanger
three ½" wide ivory ribbon roses
two ½" wide silk ivy leaves
9" of ⅛" wide pink satin ribbon
candy
low temperature glue gun, glue sticks

Tie the cherub to the basket handle so it dangles down the side; trim any excess string. Use the ribbon to make a shoestring bow (see page 9) with two 1" loops and two 1½" tails. Glue it to the handle base, then glue the roses to the bow center with the leaves extending out from behind the roses. Place the candy in the center of the tulle. Gather the corners of the tulle and tuck it into the basket.

Wedding Favors

Terra Cotta Pot
by LeNae Gerig

2¼"x2¼" terra cotta pot
14" square of ivory tulle
¾" wide pink paper rose with 1" leaf
¾" wide white paper rose with 1" leaf
¾" wide blue silk flower
8" of 1½" wide ivory satin ribbon with wired edges
10-12 mint candies
low temperature glue gun, glue sticks

1 Wash the pot and let it dry, then fill it with candy. Place the pot centered on the tulle square; gather the edges over the top of the pot and twist once.

2 Wrap the ribbon around the gathered tulle and knot it to secure the edges. Glue the roses centered on the knot, with the blue flower centered below them. Glue the leaves extending from behind the flowers.

Helpful Hint

Always check with the person in charge of the facility before deciding on your favors, as some churches and reception sites do not allow anything to be thrown, while others may charge a clean-up fee.

Designer Tip
Rice is not healthly for birds, so birdseed has replaced rice as the main tosser material.

Ivory Birdseed Tosser

by LeNae Gerig

9" square of ivory lace fabric
9" square of ivory tulle
12" of ⅛" wide ivory satin ribbon
⅜" wide ivory ribbon rose with two green ribbon
   leaves
⅛ cup of birdseed (no sunflower seeds)
low temperature glue gun, glue sticks

1 Place the tulle square over the lace square. Pour the birdseed centered on the squares. Gather the four corners together and twist once.

2 Wrap the ribbon around the gathered corners and make a shoestring bow (see page 9) with two 1" loops and two 1" tails. Glue the rose to the bow center.

Flower-Topped Bubbles
by LeNae Gerig

2" tall white plastic bottle of bubbles
three ¾" wide white cloth flowers
two 1" wide green silk ivy leaves
9" of ⅜" wide white sheer ribbon with satin edges
low temperature glue gun, glue sticks

Wrap the ribbon around the bottle neck and make a shoestring bow (see page 9) with two 1" loops and two 1" tails. Glue the ivy leaves to the top of the bottle cap, extending outward on each side. Glue the flowers centered on the leaves.

Helpful Hint

It is best to only use bubbles outside, as they can make floors slippery and dangerous for guests. If you have any questions, check with the person in charge of the facility to see which items are allowed and which are not.

Pink Tulle Bubbles
by LeNae Gerig

2" tall white plastic bottle of bubbles
two 9" wide circles of pink tulle
12" of ½" wide white satin ribbon with sheer edges
1" wide pink tulle flower with pink ribbon rose center
low temperature glue gun, glue sticks

Place the tulle circles together, then place the bottle in the center of the circles. Gather the tulle edges up over the bottle and twist once. Wrap the ribbon around the gathered tulle and make a shoestring bow (see page 9) with two 1¼" loops and two 1¼"tails. Glue the flower to the bow center.

Helpful Hint

Have your flower girl or other young attendants hand out the bubbles to your guests attending the reception, so they can blow them outside as the newlyweds leave.

BridalFlorals

Today's silk floral materials are so realistic and versatile they can easily adapt to any bridal style. While they are less expensive than fresh florals, they also are very easy to work with and, best of all, can be assembled well in advance of the wedding day. In addition, they aren't dependent upon seasons as the fresh flowers are—you can have beautiful roses any time of the year without worrying about available quantities and their quality.

To provide choices and variety, we're featuring four basic styles in this book: Pastel Garden, Jewel Tones, Romantic and Classic. Each style uses similar flowers throughout the various designs, yet all are versatile enough that substitutions can easily be made. If you find a bouquet style you can't live without, but you'd prefer different floral materials, simply substitute your flowers for those in the instructions. If you'd like the bouquet to be larger, add additional florals as you're assembling the bouquet.

Bouquets for the bride and bridesmaids are included, along with corsages, boutonnieres and accessories for the flower girls—even tosser bouquets so you're able to keep your bouquet as a momento of the event. And, because everything is made with silk and everlasting materials, you can make them at your convenience. After all, this is your wedding and you get to have it your way!

Bride's Bouquet

by Kathy Thompson

1 mixed silk floral bush, with one 2½" wide pink rose; three 2½"
   wide peach roses; lavender hydrangeas, with six 2"-5" wide clusters; four 1½"-2" pink morning glories with pink bud clusters and
   many 1½"-3" wide green leaves

1 white silk tulip stem, with 2½" long wired petals

2 stems of white silk lilacs, each with two 5" clusters of 1½" wide
   blossoms

2 stems of white silk freesia, each with three 2"-6" clusters of ¾"-1½"
   wide blossoms

1½ yards of 1½" wide iridescent lavender satin ribbon with wired
   edges

green floral tape

24-gauge wire, wire cutters

ribbon treatment on bouquet stems

1 **Freesia**—cut each stem to three 1-blossom cluster sprigs, leaving the stems as long as possible. **Lilac**—cut each stem to two 1-blossom cluster sprigs, leaving the stems as long as possible and trimming away the leaves. **Floral bush**—cut off each sprig, leaving the stems as long as possible. Slide all the leaves on each sprig up the stems to just under the blossoms. (Set aside the pink rose sprig, two 3-blossom hydrangea sprigs, 1 smaller hydrangea cluster, two 6" long freesia clusters and 1 lilac cluster for the "Garden Pastel Tosser Bouquet"; see page 66.)

3 **Adding freesias**—place one blossom to extend upward from the tulip at 12:00, 4:00 and 7:00. Add the last freesia extending out from the 9:00 hydrangea.

freesia
freesia
freesia
freesia
11:00 rose

lilacs
morning glories
roses
freesias
hydrangeas

11:00 rose
lilacs
lilacs
lilacs

2 **Tulip**—cut the stem to 14" and remove the leaves. Carefully open the tulip blossom slightly, to form a mature blossom. **Adding flowers:** with the tulip stem in your hand, add a peach rose and seed sprig at 11:00, 4:00 and 8:00. Wire the stems together tightly, just under the blossoms. Add both a hydrangea blossom and a morning glory, each centered between the 4:00 and 9:00 rose and between the 9:00 and 1:00 rose; wire the stems tightly together, just under the blossoms.

seed sprigs
11:00 rose
hydrangeas
hydrangeas
rose
seed sprigs
hydrangeas

wire here

4 **Adding lilacs**—place one blossom to the left of the 4:00 rose, one blossom in front of the 9:00 rose, and the remaining lilac to the right of the 1:00 rose. Wire the stems together tightly, just under the bossoms. Wire again around the stems 2" below the first wiring. Wrap both wired areas with the floral tape. Trim the stems to 7" below the top of the taped area. **Finishing touch:** with the bouquet turned so one set of morning glories is in front and the other set in back, glue the center of the ribbon to the back of the stems 3" above the stem ends. Bring both ribbon ends to the front, twist twice and wrap them to the back in an upward angle; repeat for two more wraps, finishing at the upper wired area. Bring the ribbon ends to the front and tie it into a shoestring bow (see page 9) with 3" loops and 6" tails.

wire and wrap

Bride's Bouquet

by Kathy Thompson

3" wide round bouquet holder for silks/drieds

1¼ yard of ⅞" wide sheer pink ribbon with gold edges

4 stems of pink/ivory silk roses, each with two 2½" wide
  blossoms, a 1" bud and many leaves

2 stems of ivory silk roses, each with three 2½" wide
  blossoms and many leaves

1 stem of white silk Queen Anne's lace, with 2-3" wide
  clusters of many ¼" wide blossoms

small handful of green sheet moss

24-gauge wire, wire cutters

low temperature glue gun, glue sticks

1 **Rose stem leaves**—cut the leaves from each pink/ivory rose stem. Cut thirty 2"-3" wire lengths. Wire and tape (see page 8) 16 large leaves. (Set the remaining leaves aside for the "Romantic Tosser Bouquet", on page 67.)

↙ *wire and tape*

2 **Large leaves**—insert the 16 larger leaves into the foam extending outward around the edge to form a 9" wide, 9½" tall heart shape; using the longer wired stems at 10:00, 11:00, 1:00, 2:00 and 6:00; the shortest stem at 12:00.

11:00   ↓ 12:00
10:00   ↗ 1:00
                    ↗ 2:00

↑ 6:00

Helpful Hint

While we used pink as the main color in this bouquet, choose colors that best represent you. And, by using silk flowers, you'll be able to make this bouquet anytime.

3 **Pink/ivory roses**—cut all the blossoms and buds from the stems to 2½" long. (Set aside three buds for the tosser bouquet.) Insert the largest blossom at 6:00, a bud at 12:00 and three on each side, evenly spaced. Insert the remaining blossom into the center. **Ivory roses**—cut all the blossoms from each stem to 2½" long. (Set aside one blossom for the tosser bouquet.) Glue five ivory blossoms evenly spaced encircling the center rose, at 6:00, 8:00, 10:00, 2:00 and 4:00.

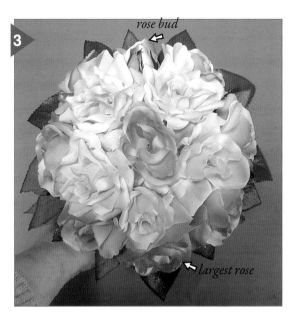

rose bud
↙

largest rose

4 **Queen Anne's lace**—cut twenty-nine 3-blossom sprigs, each ¾" long. (Set the rest aside for the tosser bouquet.) Insert five smaller rose leaves evenly spaced around the center rose. Insert 11 smaller rose leaves evenly spaced around the ivory roses. Glue the Queen Anne's lace sprigs evenly between the flowers. **Finishing touch:** tuck and glue the moss around the outer leaf stems to cover any exposed foam. **Ribbon**—cut it to one 12", two 11" and two 10" lengths. Tape a 1½" wire to one end of each ribbon. Insert the ribbons into the holder bottom extending downward, with the 12" length in the center, an 11" length on each side of it, and a 10" length outside the 11" ribbons. Trim each ribbon end at an angle.

Bride's Bouquet

by Kathy Thompson

3" wide round bouquet holder for silks/drieds
8" wide purple/blue silk hydrangea candle ring, with four 2"
   wide clusters, four 4" wide clusters and many leaves
1 plum/burgundy silk ranunculus bush with ten 1½"-3" wide
   blossoms and many leaves
1 stem of gold silk ranunculus with three 1½"-3" wide blossoms
2 stems of cream silk roses, each with three 2"-3" wide blossoms
7 sprigs of yellow dried yarrow with 2"-3" wide blossoms
2 oz. of yellow dried hanging amaranthus
small handful of green sheet moss
18-gauge wire, wire cutters
green floral tape
low temperature glue gun, glue sticks

cream roses

dried yarrow

1 **Hydrangeas**—cut the 4" clusters off the candle ring. Wire and tape (see page 8) one stem to 3" and one to 5". (Set the other clusters aside for the tosser bouquet on page 80.) Insert the 3" stem at 2:00 and the 5" stem at 9:00. **Gold ranunculus**— cut the blossom sprigs to two 5" and one 4" sprig. Insert the 4" sprig at 3:00, a 5" sprig at 11:00 and a 5" sprig at 6:00.

2 **Ranunculus bush**—cut a 1-blossom/2-bud stem to 11" and set it aside for the tosser bouquet. Cut the stems of four burgundy blossoms to 2½", 3", 5", and 9". Insert the 2½" stem into the holder center, the 3" at 12:00, the 5" at 8:00, and the 9" at 5:00. Cut the stems of four plum blossoms to 2½", 3½", 4" and 7". Insert the 4" at 3:30, the 2½" at 2:00, the 3½" at 11:00, and the 7" at 6:30.

3 **Roses**—cut a 2-blossom sprig to 7". Cut the other stem to two 2" and one 3" sprig. (Set the remaining blossom aside for the tosser bouquet.) Insert a 2" sprig on each side of the center ranunculus, the 3" sprig above it and the 7" sprig below it. Cut the hydrangeas from the candle ring; wire and tape one stem to be 3", two to be 4", and one to be 5". Insert a 4" at 9:00, the 5" at 5:00, the 3" at 1:00 and a 4" just below the right rose.

4 **Ranunculus leaves**—cut three clusters from the bush; wire and tape them to two 4" and one 3" wire. Insert them, extending outward behind the flowers, with the 3" at 4:00, the 4" at 1:00 and 7:00. **Hydrangea leaves**—cut them from the candle ring. (Set aside seven leaves for the tosser bouquet.) Tape and wire them to ten 2" wires and the rest to 4" wires. Glue five 2" stems among the center blossoms and the remaining to fill empty spaces; glue moss to cover any exposed foam.

Finishing touch: Insert the yarrow evenly spaced among the flowers. Wire and tape three amaranthus blossoms, each with a two or 3-blossom cluster. Insert one at the center bottom of the bouquet, with another 2" away on each side of it. Form each of three 10" amaranthus strands into a 3" loop with a 4" tail. Insert them around the center ranunculus blossom.

Bride's Bouquet

by Kathy Thompson

3 yards of 1½" wide white sheer ribbon with gold edges

2 yards of 2½" wide ivory floral print sheer ribbon with wired
    edges

2 stems of white silk amaryllis, each with two 5" wide blossoms,
    one 4" bud and 8 leaves

1 green silk peony stem, with one 5" wide blossom and 6 leaves

3 stems of yellow silk oncidium orchids, with many 1¼" wide
    blossoms

1 stem of yellow silk roses, with one 3" wide blossom, one 2" wide
    blossom, one 1" wide bud and many leaves

4 stems of green silk ivy, each with thirteen 1½"-2½" leaves

24-gauge wire, wire cutters

green floral tape

white silk amaryllis

yellow silk roses

1 **Amaryllis**—hold both stems together with the buds in the back; bend one blossom to extend outward on each side, one blossom extending upwards; and the other blossom extending downward to form a diamond shape. Wire the stems together, just under the lower blossom. **Ivy**—wire one stem to the left and right sides of the upper amaryllis, both extending upward.

3 **Peony**—position the stem with the blossom just right of the lower amaryllis and wire. **Remaining ivy**—wire one stem left of the lower amaryllis and one right of the peony; curve both downward over the front of the stems. Cut off any leaves below the wired area. Trim all stems to measure 17" from the wire to the stem ends, then wrap the wired area with floral tape.

wire here

wrap here

2 **Roses**—wire the stem with the blossoms in the center of the diamond shape. **Oncidium orchids**—wire one stem behind the left ivy to extend inward and upward towards the amaryllis buds. Wire the other stems to extend upward on each side of the lower amaryllis.

4 **White/gold ribbon**—Glue the ribbon center to the stem backs 7" above the stem ends. Wrap each side to the front and give them a full twist. Wrap both sides to the back and twist again. Repeat for five more twists along the front 1½"-2" apart, with the final twist resting on the wired and taped area; then tie the ribbon into a shoestring bow (see page 9) with two 3" loops, one 15" tail and one 18" tail. **Final touch:** tie the sheer floral ribbon into a shoestring bow with two 5" loops, one 16" tail and one 24" tail. Glue the bow center to the stem backs on the wired area with the bow loops wrapping around to the front.

Helpful Hint

This bouquet is designed to be carried cradle-fashion by the bride, with the main portion of the bouquet resting in her left arm.

by Kathy Thompson

1 white silk tulip stem with a 2½" blossom with wired petals
1 yard of 1½" wide iridescent lavender satin ribbon with wired
edges
green floral tape
wire, wire cutters
remaining materials from the "Garden Pastels Bridal Bouquet",
page 58: one pink rose sprig, two 3-blossom hydrangea sprigs,
one smaller hydrangea cluster, two 6" long freesia clusters and
1 lilac cluster

Designer Tip

Complete the "Garden Pastels Bridal Bouquet" on page 58 before creating this tosser bouquet. It's a great way to use all the materials and save money on your silk floral purchases.

1 **Tulip**—cut it to 12" and remove the leaves. Holding the tulip, add a rose to the lower left and wire the stems together tightly just under the blossoms. Add a hydrangea cluster at 3:00 and one at 5:00. Add the 3-blossom cluster above the tulip at 12:00.

2 **Freesias**—cut the stems into two 2-blossom and two 1-blossom/bud sprigs. Wire and tape each sprig to be 12" long. Add the 2-blossom sprigs at 6:00 and one at 10:00. Add the other two at 11:00 and 1:00. Add one lilac sprig at 4:00 and wire the stems together tightly.

3 Wire the stems again 2" below the first wired area, then trim the stems to 8". **Finishing touch:** With the tulip directly in front, glue the center of the ribbon to the back halfway down the stems. Bring both ribbon ends to the front, twist together and wrap them to the back in an upward angle; repeat for two more wraps, finishing at the upper wired area. Bring the ribbon ends to the front and tie in a shoestring bow (see page 9) with 2" loops and 4" tails.

hydrangea

hydrangea buds/blossoms

rose

hydrangea buds/blossoms

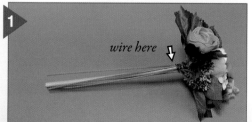

wire here

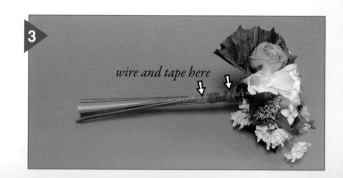

wire and tape here

by Kathy Thompson

2¼" wide round bouquet holder for silks/drieds
⅔ yard of ⅞" wide sheer pink ribbon with gold edges
1 stem of pink/ivory silk roses, with two 2½" wide
*   blossoms, 1" bud and many leaves*
2 stems of ivory silk roses, each with three 2½" wide blossoms
⅛ oz. of green sheet moss
low temperature glue gun, glue sticks
remaining materials from the "Romantic Bridal Bouquet," page
*   60: three pink/ivory rosebuds, one ivory rose blossom, twenty-*
*   two ¾" Queen Anne's lace sprigs and 22 rose leaves*

Designer Tip

Complete the "Romantic Bridal Bouquet" on page 60 before creating this tosser bouquet. It's a great way to use all the materials and save money on your silk floral purchases.

1 Wire and tape (see page 8) 14 rose leaves, then insert them into the foam extending outward around the edge, forming a heart shape. Insert the longer wired stems at 10:00, 11:00, 1:00 and 2:00, the shortest stem at 12:00, and the longest at 6:00.

2 **Ivory roses**—cut the blossoms to 2½". Insert six blossoms evenly spaced around the edge of the holder so the leaves extend behind the blossoms. Insert the other ivory rose into the center. **Pink/ivory roses**—cut the blossoms and bud from the stem. Insert two blossoms at 10:00 and 2:00, and one bud at 12:00. Insert the three other buds to complete the circle.

3 Wire and tape eight small rose leaves. Insert three evenly spaced around the center rose and five evenly spaced around just outside of the pink/ivory rose blossoms.

4 **Queen Anne's lace**—glue the sprigs evenly spaced among all the roses and leaves. Tuck and glue moss to cover any exposed foam. Cut the ribbon to one 8" and two 7" lengths. Glue the 8" centered between the 7" strips at the center bottom of the bouquet. Trim each end at an angle.

by Kathy Thompson

2¼" wide round bouquet holder for silks/drieds
3 stems of yellow dried yarrow, each with one 2"
   wide cluster
1 oz. of yellow dried hanging amaranthus
⅛ oz. of green sheet moss
18-gauge wire, wire cutters
green floral tape
low temperature glue gun, glue sticks
remaining materials from the "Jewel Tones Bridal Bouquet,"
   page 62: 1 purple/blue hydrangea
     cluster, 1 burgundy/plum ranunculus sprig with 1 blos-
     som and 2 buds, 1 cream rose blossom and 7 hydrangea
     leaves

Designer Tip

Complete the "Jewel Tones Bridal Bouquet" on page 62 before creating this tosser bouquet. It's a great way to use all the materials and save money on your silk floral purchases.

3 **Ranunculus leaves**—wire and tape two 3-leaf sprigs to 2" and three sprigs to 1½". Insert the 2" stems at 5:00 and 11:00, and the 1½" stems at 1:00, 8:00 and 12:00. Cut the remaining leaf stems to 9 single leaves; wire and tape to lengthen each stem to 2" and insert them evenly among the blossoms. **Hydrangea leaves**—wire and tape to lengthen each leaf stem to 2". Insert them around the outside behind the blossoms to fill empty spaces. Tuck and glue the moss to cover any exposed foam.

1 **Ranunculus**—cut the burgundy blossom to 3", a plum bud stem to 3" and a bud to 1½". Insert the blossom into the holder center, angled right. Insert the 3" bud at 6:00, extending downward; and the 1½" bud at 11:00, extending upward. **Rose**—insert it into the holder center, angling upward and left.

4 **Amaranthus**—cut one 4-blossom sprig to 6"; wire and tape it, then insert it at 6:00, extending downwards. Cut two 2-blossom sprigs to 5"; insert one stem just left of the rose and the other just right of the ranunculus blossom. Wire one 6" single-blossom into a loop and insert it above the burgundy ranunculus blossom.

2 Separate the hydrangea into three smaller clusters, then wire and tape (see page 8) to lengthen each stem to 2". Insert one at 1:00, 5:00 and 9:00. Cut each yarrow stem to 1½" and insert them as shown.

Tosser Bouquet

by Kathy Thompson

1 yard of 1½" wide white sheer ribbon with gold edges
1 yard of 2½" wide ivory floral print sheer ribbon with
*   wired edges*
1 stem of white silk amaryllis with two 5" wide blossoms,
*   one 4" bud and 8 leaves*
1 stem of yellow silk oncidium orchids with many 1¼"
*   wide blossoms*
1 stem of green silk ivy, with thirteen 1½"-2½" leaves
24-gauge wire, wire cutters
green floral tape

> ## Helpful Hint
> *Care should be taken when tossing this*
> *bouquet because of the sharp stem ends.*

1 **Amaryllis**—with the bud in back, bend the upper blossom outward to the right and the lower blossom upward and slightly left. **Ivy**—wire the stem right of the lowest amaryllis blossom, with the main sprig extending upward and the other sprig curving to the right.

2 **Oncidium orchids**—wire the stem in front of the amaryllis with one sprig extending left, one right and the third upward near the ivy.

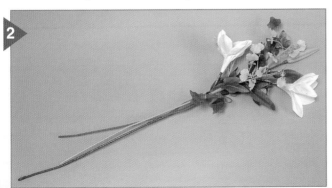

3 Wire the stems together tightly just under the lower amaryllis blossom, then cover the wired area with floral tape. Trim the stem ends to measure 10" from the wired area to the stem ends.

4 Glue the 2½" ribbon center to the back of the taped area, wrap it to the front and tie it in a shoestring bow (see page 9) with two 3" loops and 6" tails. Tie the white/gold ribbon into a shoestring bow with two 2" loops, one 9" tail and one 10" tail and glue it to the center of the other bow.

Bridesmaid Bouquet

by Kathy Thompson

1 yard of 1⅜" wide pink/lavender sheer striped ribbon with wired
   edges
3 stems of peach gerbera daisies, each with a 4" blossom
1 pink silk tulip stem, with a 2½" blossom with wired petals
1 stem of lavender silk sweet William, with five 1"-2" wide clusters
   of many ½" wide blossoms
1 stem of white silk California current, with three 2"
   clusters of ¼" wide blossoms and buds and many leaves
1 stem of green silk ivy, with thirteen 1½"-2½" wide leaves
24-gauge wire, wire cutters
green floral tape

white silk California current

1 **California current**—cut the stem into one 8", one 9" one 12" sprig. **Ivy**—cut into a 7", 9" and 12" sprig. **Sweet William**—cut the stem into a 5", 7" and 9" sprig.

2 **Tulip**—cut to 13" long and remove all the leaves. **Gerbera daisy**—cut each stem to 13". Carefully open the tulip slightly, to form a mature blossom. With the tulip in your hand, add the daisies, evenly spaced around the tulip at 1:00, 6:00 and 11:00. Wire the stems together tightly, under the blossoms as shown.

3 Add a sweet William and current sprig between each daisy pair. Wire the stems tightly, just under the blossoms. Add an ivy sprig extending upward and outward, outside each daisy; wire the stems tightly.

4 Wire the stems 1½" below the first wired area; wrap both wired areas with floral tape. Trim the stems to make the bouquet 11½" long. Cut an 8" length of ribbon. Turn the bouquet so the tulip is extending slightly left; glue one end of the ribbon to the back of the stems 4" above the ends. Wrap the ribbon around the stems, working upwards to the top wired area and glue. Use the remaining ribbon to tie a shoestring bow (see page 9) with two 2" loops and two 4" tails. Glue the bow to the bouquet front, just under the blossoms.

Bridesmaid Bouquet

by Kathy Thompson

6" foam ball

2½ yards of 1½" wide pink floral striped sheer ribbon

2 stems of burgundy/ivory silk roses, each with two 2"-3" wide
    blossoms, one 1½" bud and many 2"-3" leaves

2 stems of pink/white silk roses, each with two 2"-3" wide blossoms,
    one 1½" wide bud and many 2"-3" leaves

1 stem of ivory silk roses, with three 2"-3" wide blossoms

1 stem of white silk Queen Anne's lace, with two 3"-4" clusters of
    many ¼" wide blossoms

1 oz. of green sheet moss

U-shaped floral pins

18-gauge wire, wire cutters

low temperature glue gun, glue sticks

white silk Queen Anne's lace

1 **Ribbon**—cut a 16" length. Fold it in half to form a loop. Secure the ends with wire; trimming one wire end to 1" and the other end to 7". Apply glue along the 7" wire, then insert it through the foam center so 1" extends out the opposite side. Bend both 1" wire ends to lie flat on the ball and secure with glue. Use the remaining ribbon to make a puffy bow (see page 9) with four 3" loops, one 10" and one 11" tail. Glue the bow to the ball in front of the 8" loop, as shown.

2 **Roses**—cut all the rose blossoms and buds to 1". Set aside the stems for step 4. Glue one pink/white bud to the bow center. Glue all the blossoms and buds evenly spaced around the upper half of the ball, alternating the colors and sizes.

3 **Moss**—use floral pins and glue to cover the bottom half of the ball with moss.

4 **Leaves**—cut all the leaves from the rose stems from step 2 and glue them evenly spaced among all the flowers, extending outward. **Finishing touch:** cut the Queen Anne's lace into twenty-four 1½" sprigs, each with 3-4 clusters. Glue them evenly spaced among all the blossoms and leaves.

Bridesmaid Bouquet

by Kathy Thompson

3" wide round bouquet holder for silks/drieds
1 mixed silk bush with 3"-4" wide mauve cabbage rose blossoms, 3"-5" long burgundy/
  plum hydrangea blossoms, 1½" wide ivory rose blossoms, 1"-2" wide olive daisy
  blossoms, 4" long burgundy freesia blossoms and many 3"-4" long dusty green leaves
  (note: one bush is enough for 2 bouquets)
1 purple silk African violet bush, with a 4" wide blossom cluster and thirteen 1½"-4"
  wide dark green leaves
1 stem of navy blue silk ranunculus with three 2" wide blossoms and a 1" wide bud
1 stem of yellow dried yarrow with a 3" wide blossom cluster
handful of green sheet moss
18-gauge wire, wire cutters
green floral tape
low temperature glue gun, glue sticks

blue silk ranunculus

1 **African violet bush**—cut eight of the larger outside leaves and set them aside; cut the remaining bush with the violets and leaves to 3" and insert it as deep as possible into the holder center, angled right, as shown.

2 **Mauve cabbage roses**—cut each stem to 3". Insert the larger rose at 8:00 and the other at 12:00, both angled as shown. (Set the other two blossoms aside for a second bouquet.) **Hydrangea**—cut the lower 5" hydrangea branch into two 2½" sprigs and the upper branch into two 2" sprigs. (Set aside one of each sprig for a second bouquet.) Glue the 2½" hydrangea at 11:00 and the 2" at 5:30.

cabbage rose

hydrangeas

cabbage rose

hydrangeas

3 **Freesias**—cut the stems to measure 2½" from just below the blossom to the stem end. Insert one stem at 2:00 and 10:00, both extending outward. **Ivory Roses**—cut each 3-blossom/2-leaf sprig to 1½". (Set one cluster aside.) Insert the rose stem left of the violet. **Daisies**—cut each blossom from the bush. Wire and tape to lengthen each stem (see page 9) to 2½". (Set one full-blossom and a partial-blossom daisy aside.) Insert the daisies as shown.

roses

freesias

freesias

daisies

4 **Blue ranunculus**—cut the stem into a 2" and 3" one-blossom sprig; cut the remaining one-blossom/one-bud sprig to 3" and wire and tape it to 4". Insert the 4" sprig at 11:00, the 2" sprig at 1:00 and the 3" ranunculus at 5:00. **Finishing touch:** Cut nine leaves from the mixed bush; insert them evenly spaced around the outer edge behind the blossoms, extending outward and forming a collar. Insert eight violet leaves evenly spaced around the outer edge. Cut the yarrow into seven smaller sprigs and glue them evenly spaced among the blossoms by adhering the small stems to the leaves or petals. Tuck and glue moss to cover any exposed foam.

blue ranunculus

blue ranunculus

Bridesmaid Bouquet

by Kathy Thompson

1½" yards of 1½" wide white sheer ribbon with gold edges
1 yard of ¾" wide metallic gold sheer ribbon with gold edges
2 stems of yellow silk lilies, each with one 5" wide blossom, two 2½"-3"
  buds and many 3½"-5" leaves
1 stem of ivory silk roses with three 2"-3" wide blossoms and many
  leaves
1 stem of yellow silk oncidium orchids with many 1¼" wide blossoms
1 stem of white/green silk agapanthus with one 6" wide cluster of
  many ½"-1" blossoms
24-gauge wire, wire cutters
green floral tape

white/green silk agapanthus

1 **Lilies**—hold both stems together, with the one in front 3" lower than the other and wire them together below the lowest blossom. Angle the lower blossom slightly to the right and the upper blossom outward to the left. Position the buds as shown.

2 **Roses**—wire the stem to the lilies, with two upper blossoms upward behind the lower lily and the other blossom extending to the right behind the lower lily. **Oncidium orchids**—wire the stem behind the others, with the tallest sprig extending upward from the bouquet center and the two shorter sprigs extending outward to each side.

3 **Agapanthus**—wire the stem to the front of the bouquet, just left of the lower lily. Trim off all the leaves below the wired area, then cut all stems to measure 10" from just below the wired area to the stem ends. **Wire**—wrap wire 2" below the top wired area, then wrap each wired area with floral tape.

agapanthus

wire and wrap

4 **Ribbon**—glue the center of the 1½" wide ribbon to the back of the stems 6" above the lower ends. Wrap both sides to the front, twist them together one full turn and wrap them to the back, cross and bring them to the front. Repeat for one more twist in front and back, then bring the ends to the front over the upper wired area and tie into a shoestring bow (see page 9) with two 3" loops, one 10" tail and one 12" tail. **Finishing touch:** Tie the ¾" wide ribbon into a shoestring bow with two 2½" loops, one 8" tail and one 10" tail. Glue this bow to the center of the other bow.

Helpful Hint

This bouquet is designed to be carried in a cradle fashion by the bridesmaid, with the main portion of the bouquet resting in her left arm.

Corsage
by Kathy Thompson

2 yards of ⅝" wide lavender satin ribbon
1 pink silk tulip stem, with a 2½" blossom and wired petals
three 1"-1½" wide green silk ivy leaves
six 4" sprigs of green preserved sprengerii
26-gauge wire, wire cutters
low temperature glue gun, glue sticks
pencil, corsage pin

1 **Ribbon**—cut a 21" length. Make a puffy bow (see page 9) with a 5" center loop, two 4" loops and no tails. Use the remaining ribbon to make another puffy bow with a center loop, eight 2"-2½" loops and two 3½" tails. **Tulip**—cut the heavy stem to 1". Open the petals slightly to make a mature blossom. Wire and tape the tulip stem (see page 8) to 3".

2 Tape the eight-loop bow stem in front the tulip; then tape the two-loop bow behind the tulip. Tape the stems once more and curl the end around a pencil. Remove the pencil. **Sprengerii**—cut one sprig to 3½", four to 2" and leave the last sprig 4" long. Glue the 4" and 3½" sprengerii sprigs, extending upward from behind the tulip, with the four 2" sprigs extending outward in front of the tulip. **Ivy**—glue the leaves evenly spaced on the left side of the tulip. Insert the pin.

Helpful Hint
Make a corsage for the mothers of the bride and groom, grandmothers and guest book attendant.

Wristlet

by Kathy Thompson

1" wide metallic silver satin wrist corsage band with metal clip
1½ yards of 1⅜" wide pink/yellow striped sheer ribbon with wired edges
1 peach gerbera daisy with a 3" wide blossom
seven 1½" wide green silk ivy leaves
24-gauge wire, wire cutters
low temperature glue gun, glue sticks

Ribbon—make a puffy bow (see page 9) with eight 2½" loops and four 3" tails. Cut an inverted "V" into each tail. Wire the bow to the corsage band clip; then bend a metal tab from the clip over each ribbon tail to secure the bow. **Gerbera daisy**—cut the blossom from the stem. Glue the blossom to the bow center. **Ivy**—glue the leaves evenly spaced and extending outward from around the daisy.

Corsage
by Kathy Thompson

1 yard of ¾" wide pink/green rainbow ribbon with wired edges
3 stems of white silk lilacs, each with two-three clusters of many
*   1½" wide blossoms and many 2½"-3½" leaves*
1 stem of pink silk ranunculus with two 3" and one 2" blossom
1 stem of pink silk delphinium with three sprigs of many 1"
*   wide blossoms*
eight 3" sprigs of green preserved plumosus fern
pencil
corsage pin

1 **Ribbon**—make a puffy bow (see page 9) with six 1½"-2" loops and two 3" tails; do not cut the wire ends.
Ranunculus—cut two 3" blossoms and one 2" sprig. Tape one 3" sprig positioned over the bow center and the other 3" sprig at the upper right. Tape the 2" at the upper left of the bow. **Lilac**—cut three sprigs to 4"-6" long. Tape them evenly spaced around the ranunculus. Tape all the stems once more; then wrap the end around a pencil. Remove the pencil.

2 **Lilac leaves**—glue a large leaf to extend outward from behind both 3" ranunculus. Glue a small leaf extending upward between the two ranunculus and three evenly spaced behind the blossoms. **Delphinium**—cut three 1" blossom sprigs and glue them evenly spaced around the center ranunculus. **Fern**—glue two sprigs on each side of the center ranunculus and the other six evenly spaced extending from behind the blossoms and leaves. Insert the pin.

Helpful Hint
A wristlet can be presented to a special aunt, a friend or any female who is helping with the ceremony or reception.

Wristlet
by Kathy Thompson

1" wide iridescent white satin wrist corsage band with
*   metal clip*
1¼" yards of ⅝" wide pink sheer ribbon with gold edges
1 stem of ivory silk roses with two 2" wide
*   blossoms and many leaves*
1 stem of a pink/ivory rose with a 2" wide
*   blossom and many leaves*
1 stem of white silk Queen Anne's lace with three clusters
*   of many ¼" wide blossoms*
low temperature glue gun, glue sticks

Ribbon—make a puffy bow (see page 9) with eight 2½" loops and four 3½" tails; trimming the tails diagonally. Wire the bow to the corsage band clip; then bend a metal tab from the clip over each ribbon tail to secure the bow. **Roses**—cut the blossoms from the stems and glue them angled across the clip, as shown. **Queen Anne's lace**—cut eight ½" sprigs. Glue them evenly spaced among the roses.

Corsage by Kathy Thompson

1¼ yards of ⅝" wide gold sheer ribbon with gold edges
one 3" wide burgundy silk rose with a 1" stem
three 1½" wide ivory silk rose blossoms
sprig of three 1½"-2" wide blue silk hydrangea blossoms
green silk rose leaves: two 2", two 3"
two 6" sprigs of natural dried millet
one 5" and one 6" preserved eucalyptus sprigs
two 1½" wide clusters of yellow dried yarrow
24-gauge wire, wire cutters
floral tape, pencil, corsage pin
low temperature glue gun, glue sticks

1 **Ribbon**—make a loopy bow (see page 9) with a center loop, eight 1½"-2½" loops and two 4" tails; secure with wire, leaving a 4" wire stem. Tape it in front of the burgundy rose. Wire and tape (see page 8) each 3" leaf to a 4" stem and each 2" leaf to a 3" stem. Tape one 4" to extend upward from behind the burgundy rose and the other extending downward to the right. Tape a 3" leaf stem to each side of the rose. Tape all the ends and curl them around a pencil. Remove the pencil.

2 **Ivory roses**—glue one to the bow center and one on each side. **Hydrangeas**—glue the sprig below the center rose. **Eucalyptus**—glue the 6" sprig extending from behind the rose and the 5" just to its left. **Millet**—form each sprig into a loop and glue to secure. Glue one extending upward from behind the burgundy rose and one extending downward from behind the bow. **Yarrow**—glue both clusters to the lower left of the burgundy rose.

Wristlet by Kathy Thompson

1" wide black satin wrist corsage band with metal clip
1¼ yards of ⅝" wide metallic bronze ribbon with wired
  edges
one 2" wide plum silk carnation with two ½"-2" leaves
1 cluster of plum silk freesias with two 1"-1½"
  blossoms and two buds
two 1½" wide wine silk ranunculus blossoms
1 cluster of blue silk hydrangea with three 1½"-2" wide
  blossoms
three 1½" wide clusters of yellow dried yarrow

1 **Ribbon**—make a loopy bow (see page 9) with a center loop, eight 1½"-2½" loops and four 4" tails. Wire it to the corsage band clip, then bend a metal tab from the clip over the ribbon tails to secure the bow.

2 **Carnation**—glue the blossom to the bow center. **Freesias**—glue the cluster extending downward from the carnation. **Ranunculus**—glue one blossom right of the carnation and the other below the carnation. **Hydrangeas**—glue two blossoms below the ranunculus and the other right of the freesias. **Yarrow**—glue the clusters evenly spaced among the blossoms.

Corsage by Kathy Thompson

1¼ yards of ⅝" wide metallic gold sheer ribbon
two 4" wide white silk amaryllis with 1" stems
three 5" green silk amaryllis leaves with 1" stems
two 3" wide green silk ivy leaves with 1" stems
26-gauge wire, wire cutters
green floral tape
pencil
corsage pin

1 Wire and tape (see page 8) one amaryllis stem to 3" and the other to 6". Tape the the shorter stem in front of the longer stem. Tape two amaryllis leaves extending upward and left behind the upper blossom; tape the other leaf extending downward and behind the lower blossom. Tape an ivy leaf extending behind the top bossom at the upper right and the other extending behind the lower blossom at the lower left.

2 Use the ribbon to make a puffy bow (see page 9) with a center loop, eight 2" loops and two 3" tails; secure with wire, leaving a 4" wire stem. Tape the bow below the lower blossom, then tape all the stems and curl them around a pencil. Remove the pencil.

Helpful Hint

Corsage pins are distinctive because of their pearl heads. They're available in most florist shops and craft stores.

Wristlet by Kathy Thompson

1" wide pearlescent ivory satin wrist corsage band, with metal clip
1½ yards of 1½" wide white sheer ribbon with gold edges
two 2" wide ivory rose blossoms
three 3" sprigs of yellow oncidium orchids, each with two 1¼" wide blossoms
three 1¼" wide green silk rose leaves
26-gauge wire, wire cutters
low temperature glue gun, glue sticks

1 Use the ribbon to make a puffy bow (see page 9) with six 2" loops and four 3" tails. Wire it to the corsage band clip; then bend a metal tab from the clip over the ribbon tails to secure the bow.

2 Glue the rose blossoms to the bow center, angled as shown. Glue the orchid sprigs evenly spaced around the two roses, spreading the blossoms outward. Glue the rose leaves extending from behind the roses as shown.

Boutonniere #1
by Kathy Thompson

7 sprigs of lavender silk mini-asters, each with three ⅜" wide blossoms
1 sprig of yellow silk wild roses with two 1" wide blossoms
1 sprig of green silk ivy with four ½"-¾" leaves
green floral tape
26-gauge wire, wire cutters
low temperature glue gun, glue sticks
pencil
boutonniere pin

1 **Lavender asters**—wire and tape (see page 8) six aster sprigs to 3"-5" long. Tape all six stems together, with the taller sprigs extending upward behind the others. Cut the blossoms from the remaining lavender sprig and set them aside for step 2.

2 **Yellow wild roses**—cut to 3"; tape the stem in front of the lavender blossoms. **Ivy**—trim to 3"; tape it in front of the flowers. **Finishing touch:** curl the stem end around a pencil. Remove the pencil. Glue the three lavender blossoms to the front, as shown. Insert the pin.

Boutonniere #2
by LeNae Gerig

3 sprigs of lavender silk mini-asters, each with three ⅜" wide blossoms
one 1" wide yellow silk wild rose blossom
4 sprigs of green sprengerii fern
1 sprig of green silk ivy with two ½"-¾" leaves
26-gauge wire, wire cutters
green floral tape
pencil
boutonniere pin

1 **Lavender asters**—wire and tape (see page 8) all three lavender sprigs to 2"-3" long. Tape all the stems together, with the tallest sprig extending upward in the center. **Ivy**—trim to 3" and tape it behind the lavender blossoms, with one leaf extending outward on each side.

2 **Yellow wild rose**—trim to 3" then tape the stem in front of the lavender blossoms, extending outward to the left. **Sprengerii**—trim all four sprigs to 3"-4" long. Tape them evenly spaced behind the blossoms extending upward and outward. Insert the pin.

Boutonniere #1

by Kathy Thompson

*1 sprig of coral silk delphinium, with two 1½" wide
   blossoms*
one 2" wide ivory silk rose blossom
*one 2" sprig of white silk Queen Anne's lace with many
   ¼" wide blossoms*
*green silk rose leaves: one 3" leaf sprig with five 1"-1½"
   leaves and one 1½" leaf*
26-gauge wire, wire cutters
green floral tape, pencil
low temperature glue gun, glue sticks
boutonniere pin

1 **Delphinium**—cut the sprig to 1" long; remove
   the lower blossom and set it aside for step 2.
Flowers—trim each blossom sprig to 3"-5" long.
Leaves—wire and tape (see page 8) the five-leaf sprig
to lengthen it to 4" long. Tape the delphinium sprig
extending outward among the five-leaf sprig on the
left, the rose extending upward on the right and the
Queen Anne's lace extending upward between the
other blossoms.

2 Glue the leaf sprig extending downward from
   the delphinium. Glue the remaining delphinium
below the rose. Tape the stems once more; then curl
the ends around a pencil. Remove the pencil. Insert
the pin.

Helpful Hint

*Insert the boutonniere pin into the stem as a finishing
touch, to make sure it's ready to attach the day of the
wedding ceremony.*

Boutonniere #2

by Kathy Thompson

*1 sprig of white silk lilac with four 1½" wide blossom
   clusters*
1 pink silk rosebud with a 1" closed bud
green plumosus fern: one 4" and one 5" sprig
26-gauge wire, wire cutters
green floral tape
pencil
boutonniere pin

1 **Flowers**—trim the rosebud to 5"; two lilac
   sprigs to to 4" and two lilac sprigs to 3". Tape the
sprigs together, with the rosebud extending upward
through the lilacs. **Fern**—tape the 5" sprig extending
upward behind the lilacs and the 4" sprig extending
outward to the right.

2 **Finishing touch:** tape the stems once more,
   then curl the ends around a pencil. Remove the
pencil. Insert the pin.

Boutonnieres Jewel Tones

Boutonniere #1
by Kathy Thompson

1 plum silk carnation stem with a 2" blossom
1 burgundy silk ranunculus stem with a 1½" blossom
1 sprig of two 1½" wide blue silk hydrangea single
  blossoms
two 2" clusters of natural dried canella berries
one 3" green silk rose leaf
26-gauge wire, wire cutters
green floral tape, pencil
boutonniere pin

1 **Flowers**—cut the carnation stem to 2" and the ranunculus stem to 1½"; tape it to extend above the carnation. Wire and tape the hydrangea sprig (see page 8) to be 3". Tape it to the right of the carnation. Wire and tape the leaf to be 4". Tape it behind the flowers, extending upward to the left.

2 **Canella berries**—glue one sprig extending upward in front of the rose leaf and the other extending downward between the carnation and hydrangea. **Finishing touch:** Tape the stems once more; curl the ends around a pencil. Remove the pencil. Insert the pin.

Boutonniere #2

by Kathy Thompson

1 gold silk ranunculus stem with a 2" blossom
1 sprig of one 1½" wide blue silk hydrangea single
  blossom
one 4" sprig of nine ¼" wide artificial cranberries
one 1½" and one 2" wide dusty green/plum silk grape
  leaves
two 3" sprigs of preserved eucalyptus
26-gauge wire, wire cutters
green floral tape, pencil
boutonniere pin

1 Cut the ranunculus stem to 1". Tape the cranberry sprig fanned out in front of the ranunculus. Wire and tape the hydrangea (see page 8) to 3". Tape it in front of the cranberries. Wire and tape each leaf stem to 2"-3". Tape the larger leaf extending outward to the right from behind the ranunculus and the other extending outward to the left.

2 **Eucalyptus**—tape the sprigs extending upward behind the leaves. **Finishing touch:** Tape the stems once more; curl the ends around a pencil. Remove the pencil. Insert the pin.

Boutonniere #1
by Kathy Thompson

1 ivory silk rose stem with a 2" blossom
1 sprig of yellow silk oncidium orchids with three 1¼"
*   wide blossoms and a closed bud*
one 3" green silk rose leaf
26-gauge wire, wire cutters
green floral tape, pencil
boutonniere pin

Rose—cut to 3". **Oncidium orchids**—wire and tape (see page 8) the stem to 3". Tape it in front of the rose. **Leaf**—wire and tape the stem to 5". Tape it extending upward behind the rose. **Finishing touch:** Tape the stems once more; curl the ends around a pencil. Remove the pencil. Insert the pin.

Designer Tip

Since most silk flowers come with thick stems, we cut them, then wire and tape the stem to make it thinner and more flexible. It also makes curling the ends easy.

Helpful Hint

Make the above boutonniere for the groom, fathers of the bride and groom and the best man. Make the style below for the other groomsmen, grandfathers and other special male guests.

Boutonniere #2
by Kathy Thompson

1 green silk ranunculus stem with a 1½" blossom
*   and 3 leaves*
26-gauge wire, wire cutters
green floral tape
pencil
boutonniere pin

Leaves—cut the heavy stem of each leaf to 1". Wire and tape (see page 8) to lengthen the stems to be 3"-5". **Ranunculus**—cut the heavy stem to 1", then wire and tape it to lengthen it to 4". Tape the leaf sprigs evenly spaced around the ranunculus. **Finishing touch:** Tape the stems once more; curl the ends around a pencil. Remove the pencil. Insert the pin.

Flower Girl Head Wreath
by LeNae Gerig

1 bunch of 10 light blue silk daisies with many ½"
   wide blossoms, tiny blue berries and ¼"-½" long
   leaves
1 bunch of 10 lavender silk daisies with many ½"
   wide blossoms, tiny lavender berries and ¼"-½"
   long leaves
2 bunches of 10 light pink paper mini roses with many
   ½" wide buds and ½" long leaves
2 bunches of 10 yellow paper mini roses with many ½"
   wide open buds and ½" long leaves
1 bunch of 10 white paper mini roses with many ½"
   wide buds and ½" long leaves
2 bunches of three 1½" wide white silk roses with 1¼"
   long leaves
2 bunches of three 1½" wide light pink silk roses with
   1¼" long leaves
1 yard each of: ⅛" wide light pink satin ribbon, ⅝"
   wide sheer lavender striped ribbon, ⅜" wide light
   blue picot ribbon
green floral tape
22-gauge wire, wire cutters
measuring tape

1 Measure the circumference of the flower girl's head; add 2" to the wire and cut. Twist 1" of the wire ends together and cover the ends with floral tape.

2 **Flowers**—cut the individual flower stems to 2". Gather three or four stems together and wrap them to the wire with floral tape. Place another small cluster with the blossoms covering the stems of the first cluster and wrap with tape to secure. Repeat the process until you reach the first bunch of flowers. Leave a 1" wide space between the first and last bunch of flowers.

3 Holding all the ribbons together as one, wrap them around the 1" opening of the wire base and tie in a showstring bow (see page 9) with 2" loops and 12"-15" tails.

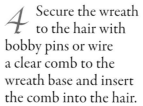

4 Secure the wreath to the hair with bobby pins or wire a clear comb to the wreath base and insert the comb into the hair.

Note: *The number of flowers needed will vary depending on the head circumference.*

Flower Girl Headband
by LeNae Gerig

1" wide white plastic headband
1 cluster of twelve 1" wide pink tulle flowers with ⅜"
 wide pink ribbon rose centers
1 cluster of twelve ivory tulle flowers with ⅜" wide
 ivory ribbon rose centers
2 clusters of twelve 1" wide pink ribbon roses
1 cluster of twelve 1" wide ivory ribbon roses
1 cluster of twelve ½" wide white ribbon roses
low temperature glue gun, glue sticks

1 Cut each flower and ribbon rose stem to ⅛".
Beginning at the center top, glue the pink tulle
flowers evenly spaced along the headband and
angled toward the front and back. Next, glue the
ivory tulle flowers evenly spaced on the headband.
Glue the remaining flowers to fill in all the empty
areas, spacing them evenly and stopping 1" from the
ends of the headband.

Willow Basket
by LeNae Gerig

7½"x3½" willow basket with 8" tall handle
six ¾" wide burgundy silk flowers
four ¾" wide green silk ivy leaves
2½ yards of ⅛" wide burgundy satin ribbon
ivory spray paint
newspapers
22-gauge wire, wire cutters
low temperature glue gun, glue sticks

1 Spray paint the basket on newspapers in a well-
ventilated work area, lightly coating the basket on
all sides. Let dry, then add a second coat. Cut an 18"
ribbon length. Glue one end to the handle inside base.
Wrap the ribbon in a spiral around the handle, gluing
the end to the opposite inside handle base. Cut the
remaining ribbon in half. Use each length to make a
loopy bow (see page 9) with ten 1½" loops and two 4"
tails. Glue one bow over each handle base. Glue three
flowers and two leaves centered on each bow.

Flower Girl Accessories

Pink & Pearls Flower Basket
by LeNae Gerig

8½"x4½" white willow basket with 7½" tall handle
2½" yards of 3mm white fused pearls
1 yard of ⅜" wide white gimp braid
1 bunch of twelve ¾" wide white ribbon roses
1 bunch of twelve ¾" wide pink ribbon roses
2 bunches of twelve 1" wide white satin and tulle flowers
    with pearl centers
1 bunch of six 1½" white tulle flowers with pearl spray
    centers
1 bunch of six 1½" white silk flowers with pearl spray centers
1 bunch of twelve ¾" wide pearlescent pink silk
    daisies, each with pearl centers, one cluster of six tiny pink
    berries and three ½"-1" leaves
1 bunch of twelve ¾" wide mauve silk daisies, each with
    pearl centers, one cluster of six tiny mauve berries and
    three ½"-1" leaves
low temperature glue gun, glue sticks

1 **Fused pearls**—cut 1½ yard. Glue one end at the handle base, drape the length loosely around the basket in a scallop pattern gluing every 4", as shown.

2 **Gimp**—glue one end of the braid to the inside of the handle base. Wrap it around the handle 7-8 times and glue the other end to the opposite inside handle base. Repeat with the remaining pearls.

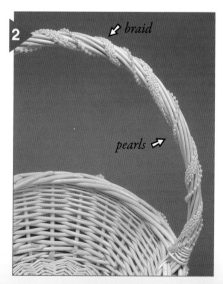

braid

pearls

3 **White flowers**— cut each flower to 1". Glue each variety in alternating angles evenly spaced around the basket rim, starting with the satin roses, following with the silk blossoms and then the tulle flowers.

4 **Pink flowers**—cut each flower to 1". Glue each variety in alternating angles evenly spaced around the basket rim among the white blossoms, starting with the satin roses, following with the pearlescent blossoms and finishing with the mauve silk flowers.

Fabric Covered Basket
by LeNae Gerig

8"x3½" bleached willow basket with 7" tall handle
two 12" white satin fabric circles
6" white satin fabric circle
4" cardboard circle
two 1½" wide white satin ribbon roses
26" of ⅜" wide ivory gimp braid
26" of 2" wide ivory crocheted lace
2 yards of ⅝" wide white satin ribbon
24" of 1½" wide ivory satin ribbon with wired edges
26-gauge white cloth covered wire, wire cutters
low temperature glue gun, glue sticks

Helpful Hint

Substitute the fabric with that of your bridesmaids' dresses for another look. Or, fill the basket with an assortment of petals matching your florals.

1 Place one 12" circle face down, with the basket centered on top. Pull the fabric up and over the basket rim, wrapping any edges to the inside. Use the glue gun to secure the edges.

2 Place the other 12" fabric circle centered face up inside the basket; glue the edges to secure. Place the 6" circle with the fabric face down and center the cardboard circle on top; bring the edges to the back of the cardboard and glue them in place. Glue the circle face up inside the basket.

3 Glue one end of the ⅝" wide ribbon to the base of the handle, inside the rim. Wrap the ribbon tightly around the handle to cover it and glue the end to secure. Beginning at the handle, glue the lace along the top edge of the basket rim, covering the raw edges of fabric. Glue the braid along the top edge of the lace.

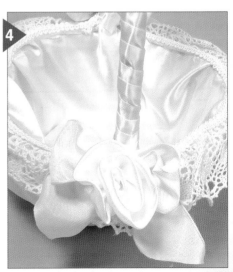

4 Cut two 12" lengths of the ivory ribbon. Use each to make a shoestring bow (see page 9) with two 1½" loops and two 2" tails. Glue one bow to the outside of each handle base. Glue a satin rose to the center of each bow.

Bridal Accessories

Satin Ring Pillow
by LeNae Gerig

two 10" squares of ivory satin fabric
11" of ⅝" wide white satin ribbon
18" of ⅛" wide ivory satin ribbon
12" of ¼" wide ivory satin ribbon
1½" wide satin ribbon roses: 2 white, 2 ivory
20" length of 3mm white fused pearls
polyester fiberfill
sewing machine, ivory thread
sewing needle
straight pins
fabric glue

Helpful Hint
If your ringbearer is very young, you may wish to place an optional pair of rings on the pillow and have the best man carry the genuine set.

1 Place one 10" square of fabric right side up. Place the ⅝" white ribbon across the vertical center of the square; pin each ribbon end to the fabric edge. Place the other 10" square of fabric right side down on the first and pin the edges together.

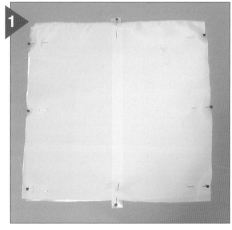

2 Stitch ¼" from the fabric edge around the square, leaving a 4" opening on one side. Remove the pins and turn the pillow right side out. Stuff the pillow firmly with the fiberfill. Fold the opening edges in and hand-stitch the opening closed.

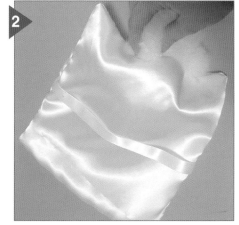

3 Insert the needle in the center back of the pillow without catching the ribbon and pull it through the center top of the pillow. Insert the needle ¼" away and pull it through the pillow to the back; pull it firmly making a small indentation. Repeat this process three more times, then knot the thread on the center back and trim the excess.

4 Use the ⅛" wide ribbon to tie a shoestring bow (see page 9) with 3" loops and tails; glue it to the center top of the pillow. Cut the stems of the four ribbon roses to ½" and glue them over the bow, alternating the colors. Cut the pearl strand into 4" lengths. Hold the ends of one length together to make a loop and glue it extending between two roses, as shown in the large photo. Repeat for the remaining strands, with the last loop extending from the center of the roses. Tie a knot in the center of the ¼" wide ribbon; glue the knot between the center of the roses. Tie the rings onto the pillow with the ribbons.

Ivory Heart Ring Pillow
by LeNae Gerig

10½" wide ivory satin heart shaped pillow with tulle ruffle and
  hand strap
18" of ⅛" wide ivory satin ribbon
two 1½" wide burgundy silk rosebuds, each with two 1"-1½" leaves
one 1" wide burgundy silk rosebud with two 1"-1½" leaves
two 1½" wide yellow silk rosebuds, each with two 1"-1½" leaves
½ oz. white preserved baby's breath
sewing needle with large eye, ivory thread
low temperature glue gun, glue sticks
(optional: two gold metal rings)

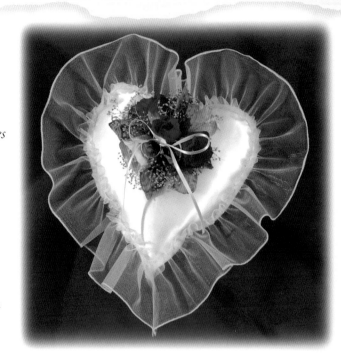

1 Thread the ribbon through the needle and make a stitch in the center top of the pillow. Pull the ribbon ends even and remove the needle.

2 Cut the leaves from the roses. Glue the 1" burgundy bud in the center, just above the ribbon stitch. Glue the other rosebuds around it as shown. Cut the baby's breath into 1"-1½" sprigs. Glue the leaves around the roses as shown and baby's breath among the rosebuds. Thread the ribbon through the rings and tie in a shoestring bow (see page 9).

Rose Petal Ring Pillow by LeNae Gerig

two 14" squares of white satin fabric
15" of ⅝" wide white satin ribbon
18" of ⅛" wide white satin ribbon
1½ yards of 45" wide white tulle
ten 2" wide pink silk rose petals
polyester fiberfill
sewing machine, white thread
sewing needle with large eye
straight pins
(optional: two gold metal rings)

1 Place one square of fabric right side up. Place the ⅝" wide white satin ribbon across the center of the square; pin each ribbon end to the fabric edge. Place the other square of fabric right side down on the first square; pin the edges together along each side.

2 Stitch ¼" from the fabric edge along each side, leaving a 4" wide opening on one side. Remove the pins and turn the pillow right side out. Stuff the pillow firmly with the fiberfill. Fold the opening edges to the inside and hand sew the opening closed.

3 Fold the tulle in half, lengthwise; place the rose petals centered between the layers. Center the petal section of tulle over the pillow top (the side without the ribbon) and scrunch the tulle to the width of the pillow; wrap both ends of the tulle to the pillow back and tie it in a knot. Fluff the tulle ends to extend beyond the pillow edges.

4 Thread the ⅛" wide ribbon through the needle's eye and make a stitch in the center top of the pillow through the tulle; pull the ribbon ends even. Thread a ring through each ribbon end, then tie a shoestring bow (see page 9).

Bridal Accessories

Guest Book Slip Cover
by LeNae Gerig

6¼"x8½" guest book
35" of 8½" wide ivory satin fabric
ivory satin flower pick with three 2" wide
* flowers with pearl centers*
5½"x3" wide white lace corner applique
1 yard of ⅝" wide white satin ribbon
six 4mm round clear acrylic rhinestones
12" of 3mm white fused pearls
1 yard of ¼" wide white satin ribbon
sewing machine, ivory thread
straight pins
iron and ironing board
tacky craft glue
low temperature glue gun, glue sticks

1 Place the fabric right side down and fold ½" in on each long side. Stitch ¼" from the folded edge. Fold ½" in from each short end of the fabric and stitch ¼" from the folded edge.

2 Place the fabric right side up and fold in each end 8" from the side, leaving a 1" open area in the center. Stitch ¼" from the upper and lower edges of the fabric.

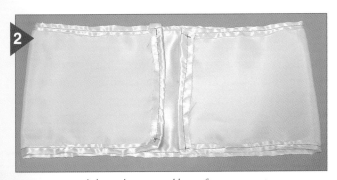

(red thread was used here for contrast)

3 Turn the pockets right side out and press with the iron. Open the guest book and insert the covers inside the pockets; then close the book.

4 Glue the applique to the upper left corner. Use the ⅝" ribbon to make a puffy bow (see page 9) with a center loop, six 1½" loops and two 8" tails. Glue it to the upper corner of the applique. Cut the flowers from their stems and glue them among the bow loops. Use tacky glue to adhere three rhinestones to the applique on each side of the bow loops. Cut the ¼" ribbon in half; hold the strips together and make a shoestring bow with four 2" loops and 3"-6" tails; knot each tail end.

Cut the pearls into two 6" lengths and fold each to form a loop. Glue the loops and bow extending from under the flowers and angled toward the lower right.

Decorated Guest Book
by LeNae Gerig

6¼"x8½" white guest book
6"x8" sheet of burgundy handmade paper
6"x8" sheet of white loose weave handmade paper
3" square of forest green handmade paper
1¾" square of metallic gold wrinkled paper
three ½" wide gold maple leaf charms
9" of gold thread
tacky craft glue
E-6000 glue
water

1 Handmade, or mulberry, papers tear easiest when wet because of the long fibers. Dip your finger into water and draw a 7" wide oval near the outer edges of the burgundy paper. While it's still damp, use your fingers to gently pull the excess paper away from the oval for feathery edges. Repeat with the white paper, creating a 5"x5½" oval. Glue the white oval centered on the burgundy oval; then use the tacky craft glue to adhere both on the front cover of the guest book.

2 Glue the gold square to the center of the white oval. Dampen the edges of the green paper and gently pull a slight amount off each side to make a 1¼" square. Glue the green square to the center of the gold square. Thread the charms onto the gold thread and tie the ends into a shoestring bow (see page 9). Fan the leaves out, slightly overlapping each other and use E-6000 to glue each to the green square.

basic black enamel frame with engagement photo

Guest Signature Frame
by LeNae Gerig

frame with mat and glass
engagement photograph
ink pens
flat-edged screwdriver

1 Remove the glass from the frame. Place the mat back into the frame and center a photograph of the engaged couple onto the mat; replace the back onto the frame.

2 Place the frame, along with several pens, on the guest table for guests to sign the mat. Add a little note explaining the frame's purpose, if you'd like. Order a wedding portrait that fits the mat and replace the engagement photo with it.

Helpful Hint

Add color to the frame by setting out gel pens representing your wedding theme.

Floral Covered Wagon by LeNae Gerig

This wagon is ideal for the toddlers in the wedding party. We suggest including a few child-safe rattles or other toys in the wagon to keep the young ones occupied and happy throughout the ceremony. A wagon can be used in most outdoor setttings, and may also be used in some church weddings. Check with the person in charge of the facility to see if a wagon would be allowed indoors.

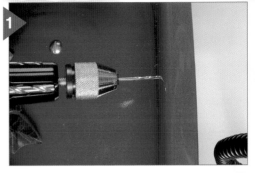

15"x33" red metal wagon
two 9" lengths of silk English ivy garlands with 1½"-2½" wide leaves
two 6" wide yellow/pink silk hydrangea blossoms
3 stems of dark red silk roses, each with four 1½" wide blossoms and
    two 1" wide buds
5 stems of yellow silk roses, each with 3" wide blossoms
4 stems of ivory silk roses, each with 3" wide blossoms
1 ivory silk rose bush with three 3" wide blossoms, three 2½" wide
    blossoms and 1" long leaves
4 yards of 6" wide white tulle ribbon
26-gauge wire, wire cutters
power drill with 1/16" bit head
black marker (to mark on metal)

1 **Drill holes**—use the black marker to mark two dots evenly spaced
1" from the top edge along both sides and one dot at the center of
each end. Use the drill to make a hole at each black dot. Remove excess
shavings.

2 **Ivy**—place the garlands around the top edge of the wagon,
securing with 9" lengths of wire inserted through each hole. Do
not cut the excess wire ends yet.

3 **Red roses**—cut the blossoms and buds to form six clusters, each
with three flowers and 3" long stems. Wire one red cluster to the
wagon front, just above the tongue, and one at the wagon back. Wire
two red clusters on each wagon side, as shown. **Yellow roses**—cut
each stem to 3" long. Wire one blossom next to each red cluster,
except in front.

4 **Ivory roses**—cut each stem to 3" long. Wire a blossom at each
wagon corner. **Ivory rose bush**—cut the six bush stems to
3" long each; wire them to the ivy evenly spaced among the other
blossoms.

5 **Hydrangeas**—separate and cut each large blossom into three
clusters. Wire the clusters next to each ivory rose blossom from
the bush. **Tulle**—beginning at the wagon front, weave the tulle ribbon
loosely among the ivy and roses.

Designer Tip

*If you have an old wagon or do not want to use a red wagon, it's easy
to create the color you want. Use steel wool to clean off any rust and
to prepare the metal surface. Spray on a coat of primer; let dry. Spray
on several coats of paint in the color of your choice, making sure to let
each coat dry thoroughly.*

Decorating for the Ceremony

Decorating for the ceremony before your guests begin arriving can be a daunting task—especially if the facility restricts the amount of time for decorating. Using silk and permanent floral materials will make this task much easier because everything can be assembled weeks in advance. Then, simply transport the finished pieces to the facility and quickly set them in place before the guests arrive.

When planning the floral designs for any facility, take into consideration the scale: if the room is very large, the floral decorations must also be large to fill the spaces adequately. Likewise, for an intimate gathering in a small facility such as a home, the decorations must be sized to fit smaller areas.

Candelabras can be found in varying sizes, so measuring each becomes key in determining the sizes of the decorations. The "Romantic" design on page 104 allows size flexibility with its three components; create the number of decorations needed, based on the size of the candelabra. And for flexibility, the single pieces can also be used as pew decorations.

The most beautiful weddings are those in which all the details, colors and styles coordinate with the setting and ceremony. With patience and planning, your wedding will be wonderful, with all the details coming together to create your vision perfectly.

Decorating for the Ceremony

by Kathy Thompson

5½"x8" terra cotta pot

1½ yards of 1½" wide periwinkle satin ribbon with wired edges

1 stem of pink/ivory silk roses, with a 5" wide blossom, a 2" wide bud and many 2"-3" leaves

3 stems of purple/lavender silk iris, each with a 5" wide blossom

3 stems of pink silk delphinium, each with a 7" long section of many ¼"-1½" wide blossoms and buds and many 2" leaves

3 stems of white silk tulips, each with one 2½" long wired-petal blossom

3 stems of peach silk gerbera daisies, each with a 4" wide blossom

1 green silk ivy bush with eighteen 9"-11" and six 18" sprigs of many 1½"-3" wide leaves

12-14 vines from an unwoven 12" wide dried honeysuckle wreath, at various lengths

handful of green sheet moss

8"x4"x3" brick of floral foam for silks/drieds

low temperature glue gun, glue sticks

24-gauge wire, wire cutters

1 For the base: cut the foam into 2 blocks. Stack them centered in the pot. Cut the 18" ivy sprigs from the ivy bush; set them aside for step 4. Coat the stem end with glue and insert it into the foam. Adjust the bush sprigs outward and upward, forming a loose ball shape at the top about 10" above the base of the stems.

2 Rose—cut the stem to 24". With one hand holding the ivy bush, slide the rose stem through the bush center and insert the end into the foam, with the tallest rose bud extending above the ivy leaves. Iris—cut each stem to 21". Slide the stems through the bush center and insert the ends into the foam at 2:00, 8:00 and 12:00. Delphinium—slide each stem through the bush center between the iris and around the rose and insert the ends into the foam. Wire the stems together once, just under the ivy leaves. Glue around the base of the stems.

3 Tulip—cut each stem to 18". Gerbera daisy—cut each stem to 18". Open each tulip, creating a mature blossom. Slide the tulip and gerbera daisy stems evenly spaced through the bush and insert the ends into the foam with the blossoms among the ivy leaves, but lower than the other flowers forming a ball shape. Wire the stems, just under the ivy leaves. Ribbon—wrap the center around the wired portion of the stems just below the ivy leaves and tie in a shoe-string bow (see page 9) with 3" loops, one 14" tail, and one 10" tail.

4 Moss—tuck and glue it to cover any exposed foam. Ivy sprigs—insert an 18" sprig into each side of the pot. Pull each upward, then cross each over the front stems to extend outward under the bow. Cut the remaining sprigs to 8"-10" lengths. Glue them evenly spaced to extend outward from the pot. Finishing touch: Insert the vines into the foam and weave them in a loose ball shape among the ivy, as shown in the large photo, with a few vines extending outward.

Decorating for the Ceremony

by Kathy Thompson

17" long natural willow gathering basket
3¼ yards of 1½" wide metallic iridescent plum/gold wired ribbon
two 2½"-3" wide feather butterflies: 1 pink, 1 ivory/tan
2 stems of pink/ivory roses, each with a 5" wide blossom, a 2" wide bud and many 2"-3" leaves
1 stem of peach/yellow silk roses, with three 2" wide blossoms and many 1"-2" leaves
2 stems of ivory/pink silk peonies, each with a 5" wide blossom
2 stems of peach silk gerbera daisies, each with a 4" wide blossom
3 stems of purple/lavender silk iris, each with a 5" wide blossom
3 stems of pink silk delphiniums, each with 12" of ¾"-1½" wide blossoms and buds
4 oz. of green preserved sprengerii fern
small handful of green sheet moss
8"x4"x3" brick of floral foam for silks/drieds
two 3" long floral picks
low temperature glue gun, glue sticks
24-gauge wire, wire cutters

rose blossom & bud

iris blossom

1 **For the basket:** glue a strip of moss across the top of the foam near each end. Place wire over the moss areas to attach the foam block centered in the basket.

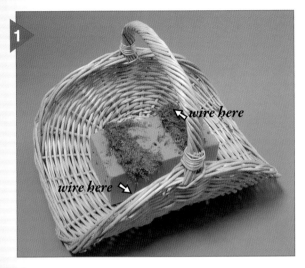

2 **Pink/ivory rose**—cut one stem to 12" and the other stem to 15" and set the stem ends aside. Insert the the 12" rose at the front of the basket and the 15" rose at the back, each parallel with the basket rim on the right. **Peach/yellow rose**—cut the stem to 10" and set the stem end aside. Insert the rose stem extending upward with the blossoms extending as shown. **Peony**—cut each stem to 4" and set the stem ends aside. Insert each blossom stem as shown. Glue the pink butterfly on one blossom. **Gerbera daisies**—cut one stem to 6" and the other to 9". Insert the 6" daisy behind the right peony and the 9" daisy extending right from behind the same peony. **Stem pieces**—insert them into the left end of the foam, evenly spaced, each extending left to represent a natural extension from the blossoms.

3 **Iris**—remove the leaves from each stem. Cut the stems to 6", 7" and 12" and shape each blossom. Insert each iris stem as shown. Insert the iris leaves evenly spaced among the flowers. **Delphinium**—cut one stem to 15" and one to 16" and the last into two 10" sprigs. Insert the stems as shown.

4 **Ivy bush**—insert it under the left peony, with the sprigs extending among the stem ends. **Ribbon**—cut a 25" length and fold it in half; wire it to a floral pick to form 11" and 13" tails. Insert the pick into the foam, with the tails extending right between the iris and rose. Use the remaining ribbon length to make a puffy bow (see page 9) with one center loop, six 5" loops and two 10" tails; wire it to the other floral pick. Insert it centered among the ivy on the left. Glue the tan butterfly to the center bow loop. **Finishing touch:** cut the sprengerii to 5"-8" lengths; insert them evenly spaced to fill empty areas on both sides of the basket.

Designer Tip

For a more natural look, bend the ivy leaves in different directions with the top sides upward.

Decorating for the Ceremony

by Kathy Thompson

12"x7"x6" light brown willow basket with 8" handle

1 dusty green silk grape bush, with fourteen 12"-14" long sprigs of many 1"-3" wide leaves, amaranthus sprigs and three 3" clusters of purple/green grapes

1 burgundy silk magnolia stem with one 7" wide blossom and two 6" leaves

2 stems of purple silk delphiniums, each with a 15" and 17" sprig of many 1"-2" wide blossoms and five 3"-4" wide leaves

3 stems of plum silk roses, each with one 4" wide blossom and 1"-2" wide leaves

1 gold silk magnolia bush, with five 3" wide blossoms

1 yard of 4" wide multi-colored velvet ribbon with wired edges (to match flowers)

8 oz. of preserved eucalyptus

8"x4"x3" brick of floral foam for silks/drieds

metallic gold spray paint

18-gauge wire, wire cutters

green floral tape

low temperature glue gun, glue sticks

magnolia bush

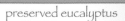

preserved eucalyptus

1 Lightly spray the basket gold; let dry. Glue the foam inside the basket. **Grape bush**—cut two 6" and one 7" sprig, each with a grape cluster; cut a 9" sprig, then cut the remainder to 4"-6" sprigs. Insert the three sprigs with grapes near the handle as shown, all draping over the rim. Insert the 9" sprig in the foam center, extendng upward left and the remaining sprigs evenly spaced, angled around the basket rim. **Amaranthus**—cut and insert the four amaranthus sprigs as shown.

2 **Delphinium**—cut one stem to 20" and the other into a 7" and 15" sprig. Insert them as shown. Cut the leaves into 3" sprigs and insert them evenly among all the greenery.

3 **Burgundy magnolia**—cut the stem to 4". Insert it into the foam as shown. **Roses**—cut one stem to 8" and the other two to 6". Insert them as shown. Cut the remaining rose leaves to 3" and insert them evenly among all the stems.

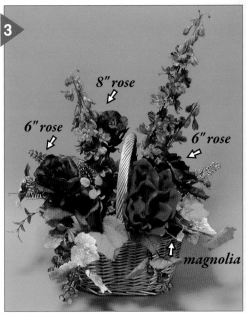

4 **Gold magnolia bush**—cut a 5", a 6" and two 7" sprigs, each with one blossom; wire and tape (see page 8) the remaining blossom to lengthen to 9". Insert the magnolia stems as shown. **Ribbon**—cut two 18" lengths. Form each piece into a 5" loop with a 7" tail and wire to secure. Glue one ribbon on each side of the burgundy magnolia, with the tails extending downward. **Eucalyptus**—cut the stems to 12"-18" lengths and insert them evenly near materials of similar heights.

by Kathy Thompson

Helpful Hint

Cluster three of these pretty bows on a candelabra as we've done here or add more to accent a larger base.

For each bow:
2 yards of 3" wide white sheer striped ribbon with wired edges
1 stem of pink/ivory silk roses, with a 5" wide blossom, a 1½" wide open bud, a ¾" wide closed bud and seven leaf sprigs
1 ivory/pink silk peony stem with a 5" wide blossom
1 stem of mauve silk ranunculus with three 1½"-2½" wide blossoms
1 stem of ivory silk gypsophilia with six 6" sprigs of 2" wide clusters of blossoms
six 9" long sprigs of green preserved plumosus fern
12" white wired chenille stem
low temperature glue gun, glue sticks

Pew Decoration: Make more bows to accent a tulle garland draped along the pew ends. Simply use the chenille stem to secure the bow to a gathered portion of the garland and the pew.

1 Use the ribbon to make a puffy bow (see page 9) with four 5" loops and two 9" tails. Secure it with the chenille stem, but don't cut the stem; it will be used to attach the bow to the candelabra.

chenille stem

2 **Rose**—cut the stem to 16". Bend the stem as shown in the pattern. Hook it over the bow center, with the full blossom centered on top and the open bud extending downward. Use the chenille stem to secure the rose stem to the bow.

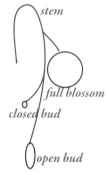

stem
full blossom
closed bud
open bud

full blossom
closed bud
open bud

3 **Peony**—cut the stem to 3" and glue it to extend just left of the rose. **Ranunculus**—cut the stem to one 5" sprig and one 3" sprig, each with a 2½" wide blossom, and one 3" sprig with a 1½" wide blossom. Glue them as shown in the photo below.

2½" ranunculus
peony
1½" ranunculus
2½" ranunculus

4 **Fern**—leave one sprig at 9" and cut the rest to 6" each. **Gypsophilia**—cut the stem into five 5" and one 6" long sprigs, each with 3 clusters of blossoms. Glue the 9" fern and the 6" gypsophilia sprig to extend downward from the peony blossom, then glue the remaining sprigs of each evenly among the flowers as shown.

Decorating for the Ceremony

by Kathy Thompson

Candelabra Swag:

2⅓ yards of 1½" wide burgundy ribbon with wired edges

2 stems of green silk magnolia leaves, each with four 5"-7" leaves

2 stems of gold silk delphiniums, each with one 7" and one 14" sprigs of many 1"-2" wide blossoms and leaves

1 burgundy silk magnolia stem, with a 7" wide blossom and two 7" leaves

2 stems of plum silk roses, each with one 5" wide blossom and leaf sprigs

1 gold silk magnolia bush, with five 4" wide blossoms

16 oz. of preserved eucalyptus

8 stems of natural dried millet: four 8", four 12"

18-gauge and 24-gauge wire, wire cutters

low temperature glue gun, glue sticks

To convert to a Reception Arrangement:

6½"x3½" ribbed terra cotta pot

gold metallic spray paint

handful of green sheet moss

3"x3"x3½" brick of floral foam for silks/drieds

Buffet Table: This arrangement can also be inserted in a container to become a spectacular reception arrangement. Container: lightly spray the terra cotta pot with gold; let dry overnight. Glue the foam in the pot, then glue moss along the pot rim. Insert the swag wires into the foam, centering the swag over the pot.

1 **Eucualyptus**—separate the stems into three groups: set aside fourteen 8"-10" sprigs for step 4, and evenly divide the remaining into two groups. Place the two bunches end-to-end, overlapping the stems to create a 38" long swag; use 24-gauge wire to secure the bunches together in the center. Attach 18-gauge wire 2" from the center on each side to form a hanger in the back.

3 **Roses**—cut the leaves from each stem and set them aside for step 4. Cut the blossom from each stem and glue one rose on each side of the magnolia. **Gold magnolia bush**—cut two 4" sprigs and three 5" sprigs, each with one blossom. Glue the 4" sprigs at 7:00 and 1:00. Glue a 5" sprig at 2:00, 8:00 and 12:00.

2 **Magnolia leaves**—cut each stem to 15". Wire the stems to the swag center, one extending toward each end. **Delphinium**—cut the lower leaves from each stem and set aside for step 4. Cut each stem to 19". Wire a stem to extend toward each end as shown. **Burgundy magnolia**—cut the leaves and set them aside for step 4. Cut the stem to 5" and bend it flat against the blossom, then wire it to the swag center.

4 **Ribbon**—cut two 18" and four 12" lengths; trim one end of each strip to an inverted "V". Tuck and glue one 18" length among the eucalyptus extending toward each end of the swag. Glue a 12" length to extend downward on each side of the burgundy magnolia; glue a 12" length angling upward from each side of the burgundy magnolia. **Millet**—glue the 8" sprigs at 1:00, 5:00, 7:00 and 11:00, extending outward from behind the burgundy magnolia. Glue the 12" sprigs at 2:00, 4:00, 8:00 and 10:00 around the center magnolia. **Finishing touch:** glue the rose and delphinium leaves evenly spaced among the other materials to fill empty areas. Glue the 14 saved eucalyptus sprigs evenly spaced among the materials extending outward and forward.

Helpful Hint

Choose someone who isn't in the immediate bridal party to transport the arrangement to the reception area for setup. Work out the details in advance, so the day of festivities will go smoothly.

by Kathy Thompson

Candelabra Bouquet:

2½ yards of 3" wide white satin-striped sheer ribbon with wired edges

2 stems of white silk amaryllis, each with two 5" wide blossoms, one 4" bud and eight 5" leaves

1 stem of ivory silk magnolias with three 3"-4" wide blossoms, one 1½" wide bud and eleven 1¼"-2½" leaves

1 green silk peony stem with a 5" wide blossom and six 4" leaves

3 stems of yellow silk oncidium orchids, with many 1¼" wide blossoms

1 green silk oak leaf bush, with twelve 10"-12" branches of many leaves

one 18" white chenille stem

24-gauge wire, wire cutters

green floral tape

To convert to a Reception Arrangement:

4"x4"x9" clear glass storage jar or vase

2 oz. of iridescent shredded packaging material

5"x3"x2" brick of floral foam for silks/drieds

Buffet Table: This bouquet can be inserted in a container to become a stunning arrangement for the reception. Place the foam inside the glass jar. Insert the shredded material around the foam to conceal it. Insert the bouquet stems into the foam and place it on the table.

1 **Oak leaf bush**—fan out the sprigs to make a circular pattern, with the longer sprigs extending downward. **Amaryllis**—place one on each side of the bush, with the blossoms extending upward and outward. Wire the stems together, 4" from the stem ends.

wire here

2 **Magnolias**—hold the stem to the oak bush stem and arange the blossoms among the bouquet as shown. Wire the stems together.

magnolia

← *magnolia*

magnolias

3 **Oncidium orchids**—arrange the stems among the materials as shown. Wire the stems together.

oncidium orchids

oncidium orchids

oncidium orchids

4 **Peony**—wire the stem to the bouquet, with the blossom extending next to the center amaryllis blossom. **Ribbon**—tie it into a puffy bow (see page 9) with two 6" loops, one 23" tail and one 26" tail. Wire the bow to the bush center. **Finishing touch:** wrap the wired area with floral tape. Trim the stems to 6". **Chenille stem**—wrap the center around several stems in the back of the bouquet and twist several times to secure; twist the ends together several times to make a loop to attach to the candelabra.

Helpful Hint

Once the arrangement is place on the candelabra, re-arrange the branches and shape the leaves. Because the sides of our candelabra angle downward, we bent the amaryllis buds downward to follow those lines. Shape the bow loops and tails at this time, also.

Lighted Arch
by LeNae Gerig

6-foot tall white metal garden arch
   (check for any additional materials
   required to assemble the arch)
two 6-foot pink and white silk rose
   garlands, each with three 5" wide
   blossoms, five 4" wide blossoms, two
   2" open buds and many 2"-2½"
   long leaves
one 6-foot yellow and white silk
   rose garland with three 5" wide
   blossoms, five 4" wide blossoms, two
   2" open buds and many 2"-2½"
   long leaves
one 25" long silk floral swag with four
   4" wide pink blossoms, four 3" wide
   pink hydrangea blossom clusters,
   three 3" wide daisy clusters, each
   with four 1¼" wide white blossoms,
   many 1"-2" wide ivy leaves, 3"-4"
   long fern sprigs and 2"-3" long rose
   and hydrangea leaves
8 yards of 54" wide white tulle
22-gauge wire
green floral tape
scissors

1 Follow the manufacturer's instructions to assemble the arch, securing each rung before proceeding with the decorations. Cut the tulle into one 6-yard and two 1-yard lengths. Gather the center of the 6-yard length and wire it to the center top front of the arch. On the left side of the arch measure 18" of tulle and secure it to the arch 12" from the top center. Arrange the excess tulle around the wired area to make a "Bishop's sleeve." Repeat down the left side of the arch for a total of four Bishop's sleeves. You will have 12" of tulle remaining. Wire a 1-yard length of tulle under the 12" for a skirted look.

2 Repeat the Bishop's sleeves and tulle for the right side of the arch.

3 Wire the center of the pink and white garland to the top front center of the arch. Wrap each end once around the tulle and arch and wire in place. Cut the remaining garlands in half. Use floral tape to secure a yellow length to each end of the pink garland. Wrap each

yellow length once around the tulle and arch and wire in place. Tape a pink length to each end of the yellow length. Wrap each pink length once around the tulle and arch and wire in place.

4 Bend the swag to slightly curve it and wire it to the center of the top front of the arch in two places. Arrange the blossoms on the garlands to face forward and maximize their impact. Fluff the Bishop's sleeves so they are not crushed by the flowers.

Designer Tip

Place this arch as a backdrop for the bride and groom at the alter or for photographs. Or use as an archway for the bridal party to walk through.

Pink Rose Garland
by Kathy Thompson

18-foot grapevine garland
two 9-foot green silk ivy garlands
2½ yards of 1½" wide metallic iridescent plum/gold
*   wired ribbon*
three 5" wide yellow feather butterflies
two 24" lavender/yellow silk hydrangea swags, each
*   with twelve 2"-3" wide flower clusters, 4 purple*
*   bud clusters and many leaves*
1 stem of pink/ivory silk roses with one 5" wide
*   blossom, one 1½" bud and many leaves*
1 stem of pink/ivory silk roses with two 2" wide
*   blossoms, one 1" bud and many leaves*
2 stems of pink/white silk roses, each with one 2½"
*   wide blossom, one 2" wide blossom, one ¾" bud*
*   and many leaves*
18-gauge wire, wire cutters
low temperature glue gun, glue sticks

arch center

1 **Ivy**—wire one end of an ivy garland at the center of the grapevine garland; wrap and weave the ivy among the vines. Repeat with the other ivy garland on the opposite end.

2 **For the center swag:** wire the center of one swag to the garland center (see large photo). **Pink/ivory rose stems**—cut the 5" rose stem to 15" and wire it to the garland center, with the 5" blossom at the swag center and the bud extending to the left. Cut the 2½" rose stem to 12" and wire it to the swag with the blossom extending to the upper right of the 5" rose. Cut the blossoms and leaves off the other 2½" rose stem and set aside.

3 **Ribbon**—make a loopy bow (see page 9) with six 5" loops, one 11" and one 12" tail. Glue the bow behind the 5" rose, with the tails extending downward.

4 **Remaining florals**—glue the 2" rose stem on the right end of the garland with the blossom 42" from the center. Glue the cut roses from step 2 on the left end of the garland to match the right. Cut all the blossoms and leaves from the hydrangea swag and glue them evenly on both ends of the garland. Glue all the leaves evenly spaced among all the materials. **Butterflies**—glue two to the left of the swag center and the other one to the right, as shown.

Decorating for the Ceremony

Pew Bow Garland
by LeNae Gerig

18-foot grape leaf garland, with many
    1"-5" wide dusty leaves and dusty
    plum grape clusters (number depends
    on aisle length)
24" wide white tulle (length depends
    on aisle measurement)
2 yards of 2½" wide white satin ribbon
    with open weave wired edges (for
    each bow)
22-gauge white fabric covered wire,
    wire cutters

Measure each aisle to determine the
length of tulle and number of ivy
garlands needed. Weave the tulle
among the garland, as shown. With
the ribbon, make a puffy bow (see
page 9) with a center loop, eight 4"
loops and two 8" tails. Cut the tails in
an inverted "V". Secure the bow with
the white wire, twisting twice. Attach
the garland to the pews, then attach a
bow to the garland at each pew.

Designer Tip

*Be sure to measure the length of each side of the aisle and add a few extra
yards before purchasing the garland and tulle. Also, allow the tape measure
to drape along each pew when measuring.*

Rose Bow Garland

by Kathy Thompson &
LeNae Gerig

*108" wide white tulle
rose bow materials (see page 104)*

1 Determine the number of
    rose bows you need to make,
based on the number of pews to be
decorated. Measure the length of
the aisle and add several yards to
determine the length of tulle needed
for each side.

2 Gather and drape the tulle
    along the pew ends, twisting
it once between each pew pair. Use
the chenille stem on the rose bow to
attach the bow to the pew.

Garden Pastels Floral Clip

by Kathy Thompson

7" long plastic pew clip
1½ yards of 1⅜" wide pink/yellow sheer striped ribbon
   with wire edges
10" wide candle ring with a 7" wide holder, eight 2"-4"
   wide clusters of many 1"-1½" wide blue/lavender silk
   hydrangeas blossoms and many leaves
1 stem of peach/yellow silk roses with three 2" wide
   blossoms and many 1"-2" leaves
1 stem of pink silk delphinium, each with a 12" section
   of ¾"-1½" wide blossoms and buds
12 dried honeysuckle vines from a 12" wreath
24-gauge wire, wire cutters
low temperature glue gun, glue sticks

1 **Candle ring base**—cut the ring in half, with four blossoms on each half. Bend the half ring into a circle and secure with wire. Use more wire to secure the ring to the pew clip in two places.

wire here

wire here

2 Tie the ribbon in a shoestring bow (see page 9) with two 5" loops, one 10" tail and one 12" tail. Wire the bow to the ring top with the tails woven among the leaves around the ring.

10" tail

12" tail

3 **Rose**—cut each blossom and leaf sprig from the stem. Glue the largest blossom at the bow center, then glue one at 4:00 and one at 5:00. Glue the rose leaves extending outward from behind the hydrangea leaves.

larger rose

4 **Delphinium**— cut the blossoms from the stem and glue them evenly among the flowers. **Vines**—cut them to 20"-24". Loop the vines among the blossoms and leaves and glue to secure.

delphinium

Pew Decorations

by Kathy Thompson

7" long plastic pew clip, with foam cage for silks/drieds
⅔ yard of 1½" wide iridescent rust satin ribbon with gold
    wired edges
green silk hibiscus leaf stem, with eight 4" leaves
1 burgundy silk magnolia stem with a 7" wide blossom and
    two 6" leaves
1 stem of navy blue silk ranunculus, with three 2½" wide
    blossoms and one 1" bud

1 stem of gold silk delphinium, with 7" and 15" sprigs of
    many 1"-2" wide blossoms and five 3"-4" leaves
four 13" long stems of natural dried millet
3 oz. of preserved eucalyptus
⅛ oz. of green sheet moss
18-gauge wire, wire cutters
green floral tape
low temperature glue gun, glue sticks

114

1 **Eucalyptus**—cut ten 7"-9" and six 5"-6" sprigs. Insert the longer sprigs evenly spaced around the outside of the foam cage, as shown. Insert the 5"-6" sprigs evenly spaced into the foam center, angled upward. **Hibiscus**—cut two leaves to 7" and the others to 6". Insert two 6" leaves into the center at 3:00 and 9:00, extending forward. Glue the remaining leaves as follows: a 7" leaf at 5:00 and 11:00; a 6" leaf at 1:00, 4:00, 7:00 and 10:00.

eucalyptus

hibiscus

2 **Magnolia**—cut the stem to 2"; insert it into the center. **Magnolia leaf**—cut each stem to 1"; insert one at 1:00 and 7:00, extending outward. **Millet**—form the stem into a 3" loop with a 3" stem (see page 8 for stem bending technique); use floral tape to secure. Repeat with the other millet stems. Insert two left of the magnolia at 10:00, angled upward and two right of the magnolia at 4:00, angled downward.

millet

millet

3 **Ribbon**—cut it in half. Fold one length in a loop and secure it with wire, leaving 3" wire tail. Wrap a 3" wire length around one end of the other length; cut an inverted "V" into the opposite end. Insert the wired ends into the foam, positioning the loop near the upper millet and the tail near the lower millet as shown. **Ranunculus**—cut the stem to one 4" one-blossom, one 5" one-blossom and one 5" blossom/bud sprig. Insert the 4" sprig right of the magnolia at 3:00. Insert the 5" one-blossom at 1:00 and the other sprig at 2:00.

ranunculus

4 **Delphinium**—cut the 15" sprig to 12" and 2"; remove the four lower blossoms from the 12" sprig. Wire and tape the 2" sprig to lengthen it to 4". Cut the 7" sprig with one leaf from the stem. Cut the remaining leaves from the stem. Insert the delphinium sprigs as shown, tucking the single blossoms among the flowers and leaves. **Finishing touch:** Insert a delphinum leaf behind each single blossom. Tuck and glue moss to cover any exposed foam.

12" delphinium

7" delphinium

single delphinium

4" delphinium

Pew Decorations

by Kathy Thompson

7" long plastic pew clip, with foam cage for silks/drieds
2 yards of 1½" wide white sheer ribbon with gold edges
1 stem of ivory silk magnolias, with three 3"-4" wide blossoms,
   one 1½" wide bud and eleven 1¼"-2½" leaves
1 stem of yellow silk oncidium orchids, with many 1¼" wide
   blossoms

1 green silk ivy bush, with many 6"-14" branches
   of ¾"-2" leaves
9" tall white plastic battery-operated candle lamp
2 AA batteries
⅛ oz. of green sheet moss
24-gauge wire, wire cutters
low temperature glue gun, glue sticks

yellow silk oncidium orchids

ivory silk magnolia blossoms

1 **Candle lamp**—unscrew the base from the candle. Insert the candle bottom into the top of the foam cage so the candle top is slightly taller than the top portion of the pew clip; glue to secure.

2 **Ivy bush**—cut each branch from the bush. Insert the longer branches evenly spaced into the foam cage bottom. Insert the medium length sprigs evenly spaced into each foam side, all extending outward; insert the shorter sprigs into the foam top, extending upward and forward.

3 **Magnolias**—cut the stem to one 6" one-bud, two 3" one-blossom and one 4" one-blossom sprig. Insert the 4" blossom into the foam center, one 3" blossom above and left of the center, and the other 3" blossom above and right of the center. Insert the 6" bud into the bottom left of center, extending downward. **Oncidium orchids**—cut the stem to 12". Insert it behind the center magnolia, with a sprig extending outward to each side and the other sprig extending downward.

4 Tuck and glue moss to cover any exposed foam. **Ribbon**—cut a 27" length. Fold it in half and secure with wire to form two tails; insert the wire into the bottom. Cut an inverted "V" into each tail end. **Finishing touch:** cut the remaining ribbon in half. Make each length into a puffy bow (see page 9) with two 4" loops and no tails. Glue one bow on each side of the center magnolia.

Helpful Hint

Insert fresh batteries in the holder and test each candle to make certain the connections work before the wedding day.

Unity Candles

by Kathy Thompson

3 terra cotta pots: two 3¼"x3", one 4"x5"
2 taper candle and 1 pillar candle green plastic candle spikes
two 10" white taper candles
2½"x9" white pillar candle
3¼" long white/mauve/brown bird
3" wide twig nest
2½ yards of 1⅜" wide lavender striped sheer ribbon with wired edges
one 8" wide mixed silk floral candle ring, with ivory/peach
    hydrangeas, coral and peach ranunculus, a peach/yellow lily, white dogwood
    blossoms, an ivory camellia, a peach freesia, a cluster of ivory lilacs and
    various leaves
two 4" wide mixed silk floral candle rings, with tivory/peach hydrangeas, coral
    ranunculus, an ivory camellia, a cluster of ivory lilacs and various leaves
3 stems of lavender silk lilacs, each with three 4½" long clusters of many ½"-1"
    wide blossoms
2 stems of white silk freesias, each with two 3" and one 5" long sprigs of ¾"-
    1½" wide blossoms and buds
⅛ oz. of green sheet moss
honeysuckle vines from a 12" wide wreath
floral foam for silks/drieds: two 2"x2"x2" and one 4"x4"x3" block
24-gauge wire, wire cutters
low temperature glue gun, glue sticks

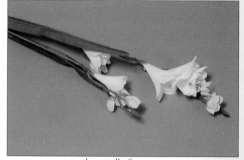

white silk freesias

dried honeysuckle vine wreath

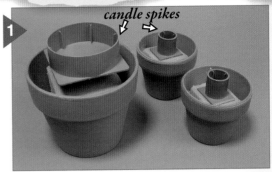

candle spikes

1 **For the bases:** trim the large foam brick to fit inside the large pot; glue the pillar candle spike centered on the foam. Trim each smaller foam brick to fit inside a small pot, then glue a taper candle spike on the foam in each small pot.

2 **Floral candle rings**—cut a slit in the large ring to slide it over the pillar candle spike. Repeat the process with the two smaller rings for each small pot.

3 **For the larger pot:** cut one freesia stem into two 6" and an 8"sprig. Glue them extending over the rim, with the 6" sprigs at 3:00 and 6:00 and the 8" sprig at 9:00. **Lilacs**—cut one stem into three 6" sprigs, each with one blossom cluster. Glue the sprigs extending over the rim at 1:00, 4:00 and 7:00.

freesia

freesia

freesia

lilac sprig

lilac sprig

4 Cut a 1½-yard ribbon length and make a puffy bow (see page 9) with four 4" loops and two 9" tails. Glue the bow to the lower base of the pot, at the 5:00 position. Glue a 1½" square of moss centered in the nest and the bird on top of it. Glue the nest to the bow center, gluing the back side of the nest to the pot. Glue moss to cover any exposed foam. Cut the vines into 5"-18" lengths; set half aside for the smaller pots. Glue the remaining vines among the blossoms, with the smaller vines extending upward. Insert the pillar candle into the candle spike.

peach hydrangea

peach hydrangea

5 **For each smaller pot:** cut the two lilac stems into six 3" sprigs of blossoms. Cut the two 3" freesia sprigs off the stem, then cut the 5" sprig into two 1-blossom and two 2-blossom sprigs. Glue three lilac sprigs, a 3" freesia sprig, one 1-blossom and a 2-blossom freesia sprig evenly spaced in each smaller candle ring, with the blossoms extending over the rim. Cut two 12" ribbon lengths and form each into one 3" loop with a 4" tail; secure each with wire. Insert one bow into one side of each smaller pot. Tuck and glue moss to cover any exposed foam. Glue vines among the blossoms, with the smaller vines extending upward. Insert the taper candles into the candle spikes.

lilac

freesia

lilac

lilac

freesia

freesia

freesia

lilac

lilac

lilac

Designer Tip

Ribbon loop bows are easy to make. Form the desired length loop, then fold the tail upward behind the loop. Wrap wire ½" from the folds to secure. cut the tails diagonally or in an inverted "V".

ribbon loop bow

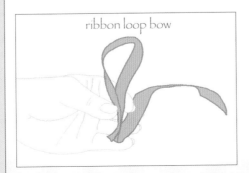

Unity Candles

by Kathy Thompson

one 4½" tall and one 6" tall clear glass taper candleholders
5" tall clear glass taper candleholder with 3¾" wide base
4½" wide clear glass pillar candle plate
two 10" white taper candles
2½"x6" white pillar candle
2¾ yards of 2" wide pink floral-print sheer ribbon with satin edges
2 stems of white silk lilacs, each with two 5" clusters of many 1½" wide blossoms
½ oz. of preserved plumosus fern

24" long silk floral swag, with a 4" wide pale yellow rose, a 2" wide pink rose, a 2" wide peach rose, four 3"-4" wide clusters of ivory/burgundy hydrangeas with 1" wide blossoms and many 2" leaves
24-gauge wire, wire cutters
E-6000 glue
low temperature glue gun, glue sticks

1 To make the pillar base, use the E-6000 to glue the glass candle plate to the top of the 5" tall candleholder; let dry overnight. Turn it upside down and place the pillar candle on it. Cut each lilac stem to 16". Wire one stem to the swag center, extending outward on each side. Bend the swag in a loose "S" shape, with the left side forward and the right side back.

2 Cut a 1-yard length of ribbon; weave and glue the ribbon among the swag leaves and blossoms. With the remaining ribbon, tie a puffy bow (see page 9) with four 4" loops, one 10" tail and one 11" tail. Glue the bow to the center back of the pale yellow rose, with the 10" tail extending to the right and the 11" tail extending to the left.

3 Cut the fern to 4"-5" sprigs. Glue them evenly spaced among the swag blossoms. Lay the swag on the table; set the pillar candle in front of the right end of the sway. Place the candles as shown.

Pearl-Studded Unity Candle
by LeNae Gerig

3"x9" white pillar candle
two 10" white taper candles
wedding invitation
oval template (large enough to frame the text
    on the wedding invitation)
⅜" wide white gimp braid (you'll need
    enough to cover the edge of the oval)
24" length of ⅝" wide white satin ribbon
4¼ yards of 3mm white fused pearls
50 straight pins with large white heads
5" wide white china pillar candle dish, with
    white raised dots
two 2½" tall clear glass taper candleholders
liquid acrylic sealer
wire cutters
¼" wide flat paintbrush
tacky craft glue
low temperature glue gun, glue sticks

1   **For the pillar candle:** Use the paintbrush to apply a ½" wide coat of sealer around the top and bottom edges of the candle and let it dry. Clean the brush. Use the brush to apply a layer of glue on the sealed portions of the candle. With the candle upright, wrap the pearls around the bottom base four times and cut the excess. Turn the candle upside down and repeat the remaining pearl strand around the top edge four times and cut off the excess. Straighten the rows, then let the candle dry thoroughly.

2   Place the oval template centered over the text on the invitation. Trace around the pattern and cut it out. Glue the gimp braid along the edge. Cut the straight pins to ½" lengths. Position the oval onto the pillar candle and press eight straight pins evenly spaced around the gimp to secure it to the candle. Insert 25 more pins evenly spaced over the sides of the candle. Place the candle on the dish.

3   **For the taper candles:** Apply a ¾" wide band of sealer 1½" from the bottom of each candle; let it dry. Apply glue to the sealed area, then wrap the pearls around each taper candle 5 times; cut the excess and let dry. Insert half of the remaining pins evenly spaced around the sides of each tapered candle. Place the candles in the glass holders. Cut the ribbon in half and wrap a piece around each candleholder; tie in a shoestring bow (see page 9) with 1½" loops and tails.

Designer Tip

If you have difficulty finding a dish with the raised dots, an alternate design, such as an iridescent or translucent finish, would work wonderfully. You could also apply an iridescent finish to a dish or a thin layer of transparent glue, then add glitter.

Reception Decorations

While the cake is often the star decoration of the reception, the flower arrangements bring the mood and feeling of the wedding ceremony to the reception festivities. When thinking ahead to making the decorations for the reception, consider creating pieces for the wedding that can do double-duty at the reception; this can relieve the budget quite a bit!

The table centerpieces for the buffet and guest tables can be assembled well in advance, using silk and permanent florals, and will leave you free to enjoy your day. To save time, create the smaller decorations for the guest tables assembly-line fashion. Purchase all the flowers and materials, then create all the centerpieces at one time (perhaps your attendants can help.)

Store the finished pieces in a protective box or a safe area, then transport all of them to the reception facility just before the wedding. If there are to be any last minute adjustments to the decorations requiring tools, place those tools with the decorations when they're made so they aren't left behind when it's time to decorate.

Planning ahead can eliminate frustrations as the wedding day draws near and will allow you to enjoy all the festivities. Best of all, with a minimum of work and worry, your reception will be beautiful!

Reception Decorations

by Kathy Thompson

7"x8" white resin urn
5"x5" white resin cherub planter
2⅔ yards of 1½" wide pink floral striped sheer ribbon
six 27" stems of pink silk delphinium, each with 6" sprigs of ¼"
    wide tan blossoms, and a 12" sprig with many ¾"-1½" wide
    pink blossoms
three 28" stems of white silk lilac, each with a 9" and 15" long
    sprig of many 1½" wide blossoms
two 22" stems of ivory/pink silk peonies, each with a 5" wide
    blossom and six 4" leaves
two 26" pink silk rose stems, each with 5"-8" sprigs, a 3" wide
    blossom and many 1½"-2" leaves
12" wide honeysuckle wreath
4"x4"x3" brick of floral foam for silks/drieds
E-6000 glue
U-shaped floral pins
low temperature glue gun, glue sticks

For candleholders:

two 9" round white crocheted doilies with scalloped edges
2 yards of 1½" wide pink floral striped sheer ribbon
two 5"x5" white resin cherub planters
two 4" square clear glass candle dishes
two 2½"x9" white pillar candles
two 4"x4"x3" bricks of floral foam for silks/drieds

For the Reception::

Insert a foam brick into each cherub planter. Place a doily centered on each planter, with a glass dish on top. Set the pillar candle in the glass dish. Cut the ribbon in half. Wrap each ribbon around the candle and tie in a shoestring bow with 3" loops and 4" tails. Arrange the candleholders as shown in the above photo.

1 **For the base:** with the urn turned upside down, use the E-6000 glue to attach the cherub planter upright on the urn; let dry overnight. Glue the foam to fit inside the planter. **Vines**—unwind the wreath; set aside half the vines for step 4. Insert the ends of a twig on opposite sides of the urn to make an arch; repeat with the remaining twigs to form a 12" tall dome.

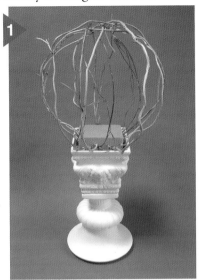

2 **Peonies**—cut each stem to 2". Insert them into the ball center. **Roses**—cut the stems to three 2", one 3" and one 5" sprig, each with 1 blossom. Insert three roses as shown in the photo and two behind the back peony. **Ribbon**—cut the ribbon in half and tie two puffy bows (see page 9); one with three 3" loops, a 5" and 8" tail, and the other with four 3" loops, a 7" and 10" tail. Glue the 3-loop bow under the roses at the left and the 4-loop bow at the right. Insert the remaining leaves from the roses and peonies evenly spaced among the blossoms, filling any empty spaces.

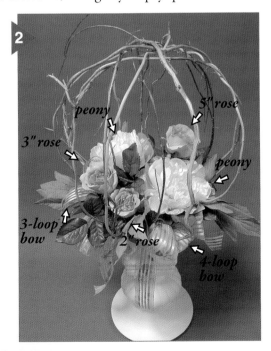

3 **Lilacs**—cut two stems to 19". Insert them into the left side, one to extend upward among the vines and the other to curve downward over the urn rim. Cut the last stem to 14" and insert it in the right side to curve downward.

4 **Delphinium**—cut four stems to 17". Insert one at the left back corner and three stems evenly spaced on the right side, all extending upward among the vines. Cut another delphinium stem to 15" and insert it at the right, extending over the urn side. Cut the last delphinium stem into one 7", one 10" sprig, and the bud sprig. Insert the 7" sprig to the right front and the other two sprigs evenly spaced on the left side of the urn. Insert twigs to fill in the empty areas around the dome and to extend over the urn sides evenly.

Reception Decorations

by Kathy Thompson

3 terra cotta pots: 4"x4", 4½"x5½", 6"x5½"

one 8" round and one 10" round terra cotta saucer

1 dusty green silk ivy bush with five 6", one 12", five 18" and
    seven 4" branches of many 1"-2" leaves

1 stem of purple/blue silk delphinium with a 10" and a 16"
    sprig of many ½"-2" wide blossoms

1 navy blue silk hydrangea bush with seven 5" wide blossom
    clusters

2 gold silk magnolia bushes, each with five 3" wide blossoms

1 stem of wine/purple silk pansies with seven 1½"-2" wide
    blossoms and many 1½"-2" leaves

three 2" wide dried pomegranates

ten 5"-10" stems of yellow dried amaranthus

ten 4"-5" stems of natural dried canella berries

½ oz. of green sheet moss

floral foam bricks cut to these measurements:
    eight 4"x1½"x1½" and one 4"x3"x2"

gold metallic spray paint

low temperature glue gun, glue sticks

E6000® glue

masking tape

green floral tape

20-gauge wire, wire cutters

serrated knife

1 **For the 3-tier base:** with the spray paint, lightly paint each terra cotta piece, allowing some color to show through; let dry overnight. Use the E-6000 to glue the pots stacked in this order: upside down 6" pot; upright 10" saucer; upside down 4"x4" pot; upright 8" saucer; and upright remaining pot. Let the pieces dry for several hours. Trim the smaller foam pieces and glue four per saucer, then the larger piece in the top pot. Use a piece of masking tape to mark 12:00 on each tier. **Ivy bush**—cut it into five 6", two 18" and the rest into 2" sprigs. **Delphinium**—cut into a 10" and a 16" sprig. **Hydrangea**—cut each cluster stem to 3". **Magnolia**—cut the stems to one 7" and nine 2", each with one blossom. **Pansy**—cut to seven 4" sprigs, each with one blossom and some leaves. **Pomegranates**—cut two 2" and one 4" stem. **Berries**—cut eight stems to 3".
Amaranthus—separate nine stems, each with 3-4 clusters; wire and tape the stems (see page 8) to 2"-3" each.

top view

2 **Bottom tier:** working in a clockwise manner, insert 6" ivy sprigs at 12:00, 4:30, 9:00 and 10:30; a two-leaf sprig at 11:30 and nine 2" sprigs evenly spaced around the tier. **Hydrangea clusters**—insert at 2:00, 4:00, 7:00 and 11:00. **Magnolias**—insert 2" sprigs at 1:00, 3:30, 6:30 and 10:00. **Pansies**—insert one at 3:00, 5:30, 8:30 and 12:00. **Berries**—insert a cluster at 3:00, 4:30, 7:00, 9:00 and 11:30, all extending downward. **Amaranthus**—insert a stem at 12:30, 4:00 and 7:00, to drape downward. Bend the ivy leaves to cover any empty areas.

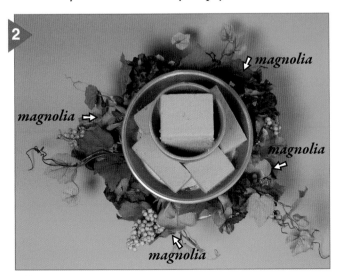

magnolia
magnolia
magnolia
magnolia

3 **Middle tier:** working clockwise, insert one 6" ivy sprig at 3;00 and ten 2" sprigs evenly spaced around the tier, bending the leaves to cover any empty spaces. **Hydrangeas**—insert one at 4:00, 7:00 and 10:00. **Magnolias**—insert 2" sprigs at 5:30, 9:00 and 11:00. **Pansies**—insert one at 1:30. **Berries**—insert a cluster at 12:30 and 6:30, angled downward. **Amaranthus**—insert a cluster at 2:30, 5:45 and 7:30. **Pomegranates**—insert a 2" and a 4" together at 8:00.

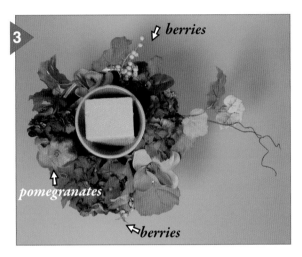

berries
pomegranates
berries

4 **Top tier:** work from the center. Insert the 16" delphinium in the foam center with the 10" stem left of it. Insert the 7" and a 2" magnolia right of the delphiniums and a 2" left of them. Insert a pansy left of all the stems and one in front of them. Insert the pomegranate left of the pansies. Insert three canella sprigs evenly around the flowers, angled over the pot edge. Insert three amarantus stems evenly around the rim. Insert one long ivy sprig left of the delphiniums and six small sprigs evenly spaced among the materials.

Finishing touch: Remove the masking tape; Tuck and glue moss to cover any exposed foam. For placement at the reception, place the two 18" ivy sprigs on the table, extending out from each side of the lower tier as shown in the large photo on page 126.

Reception Decorations

by Kathy Thompson

For lemon vase bouquet:

10" clear glass vase

7½" tall clear glass cylinder vase

1¾ yards of 3" wide ivory striped sheer ribbon with wired edges

4 stems of white silk amaryllis, each with two 5" wide blossoms, one 4" bud and eight 5" leaves

3 stems of green silk oak leaves, each with eleven 2"-4" leaves

3 stems of ivory silk magnolias with three 3"-4" wide blossoms, one 1½" bud and eleven 1¼"-2½" leaves

1 stem of yellow silk roses with one 3" wide blossom, one 2" wide blossom, one 1" bud and many 1½"-2½" leaves

4 stems of yellow silk oncidium orchids with many 1¼" wide blossoms

two 31" branches of natural dried curly willow

green floral tape

24-gauge wire, wire cutters

E6000® glue

fresh lemon slices and water

For accessory jars:

two 4"x4"x5" clear glass storage jars with lids

two 4"x4"x7" clear glass storage jars with lids

6 yards of 1½" wide white sheer ribbon with gold edges

four 4"x4"x2½" fluted clear glass votive cups

4 white votive candles

two 1½" wide yellow silk floral candle rings, each with two ¾"-1¼" wide ranunculus blossoms, one 3" wide cluster of 1½" wide hydrangea blossoms, two 1½"-2" wide ivy leaves, one sprig of five ½" wide lily of the vally and a three-leaf sprig

½ oz. of iridescent shredded packaging material

fresh lemon slices and water

1 **Amaryllis**—cut one stem to 28" and the other three to 25". Insert the tallest stem into the large vase center and the other three evenly spaced around it. **Oak leaves**—insert the stems evenly around the center amaryllis.

2 **Magnolias**—cut each stem to 19". Insert a stem in front of each oak leaf stem. **Roses**—insert the stem into the vase center. **Oncidium orchids**—cut each stem to 22". Insert them evenly spaced around the other stems. **Willow**—insert both branches into the vase center, extending upward.

3 **Wiring the arrangement**—carefully lift the stems out and squeeze them together; wire them tightly about 6" above the stem ends to secure, then wrap the wired area with floral tape. **Cylinder**—use the E6000® glue to adhere the bottom of the cylinder centered inside the vase; let dry overnight. Insert the arrangement into the cylinder, trimming the ends if necessary. **Ribbon**—wrap the center of the ribbon around the vase neck and tie it into a shoestring bow (see page 9) with two 3" loops, one 7" tail and one 9" tail.

4 **For the accessory jars (see large photo):** cut the white/gold ribbon into four 1½-yard lengths. With the lids off each jar, wrap a length around each neck and tie in a shoestring bow with two 2" loops and 5" tails. **Shredded material**—insert half into the each jar, then place a floral candle ring inside the jar. Set the lid upside down on the jar, a votive cup on it and a candle inside the cup.

For the Reception:

Just before the reception, fill the vase 1" below the top edge of the center cylinder with water and thick slices of fresh lemons. Fill the two small storage jars with water and lemons as well. Arrange the large vase in the center of the table with the 7" and 5" jars spread along the table sides, as shown in the large photo on page 128.

Reception Decorations

by Kathy Thompson

3½"x6½" ribbed terra cotta pot
3" wide twig nest
5½" mauve/blue mushroom bird
1 stem of pink/ivory roses with two 2"-3" wide blossoms, 1" wide bud
   and leaves
2 stems of purple/lavender silk iris, each with a 5" wide blossom
2 stems of peach silk gerbera daisies, each with a 4" wide blossom
2 stems of white silk lilacs, each with two 5" long clusters of blossoms
1 stem of yellow silk baby's breath with many ¼"-½" wide blossoms
½ oz. of dried honeysuckle vines from a 12" wreath
small handful of green sheet moss
4"x4"x3" brick of floral foam for drieds
low temperature glue gun, glue sticks
serrated knife

peach silk gerbera daisy

1 **For the base:** trim the foam and glue it centered in the pot. Glue the moss inside the nest, then glue the bird on the moss. Glue the nest centered on the foam.

2 **Iris**—cut each stem to 3". Cut the center three petals from each iris; twist the ends together to form two 3-petal blossoms. Insert the 3" blossoms at 2:00 and at 8:00, each extending over the rim. Insert the 3-petal blossoms next to the nest at 4:00 and at 10:00. **Gerbera daisies**—cut each stem to 2½". Insert one daisy at 1:00 and the other at 6:00.

iris

gerbera daisy

iris

iris

iris

gerbera daisy

3 **Roses**—cut the stem into sprigs as follows: the bud to 3½" long, the 2" blossom to 3" long, and the 3" blossom to 2" long. Insert the bud sprig at 9:00, the 2" blossom at 5:00 and the 3" blossom at 2:00. **Lilacs**—cut each stem into two 6" sprigs, each with a cluster. Insert one extended downward over the rim at 1:00, one at 3:00, one at 7:00 and the last one at 11:00.

lilac

lilac

rose bud

rose

lilac

lilac

4 **Leaves**—cut the remaining leaves from the lilac and rose stems. Insert the larger leaves extending outward over the rim from under the blossoms and the smaller leaves extending upward among the blossoms. **Baby's breath**—cut the stem into nine 3" sprigs. Insert them evenly spaced among the blossoms and leaves. **Finishing touch:** cut the honeysuckle vines into 6"-14" sprigs. Insert the ends into the foam, allowing the vines to loop and curl among and over the flowers.

baby's breath

baby's breath

baby's breath

baby's breath

Floral Flowerpot
by Kathy Thompson

4"x4"x5½" tan floral pot with green floral foam insert
2 yards of ¾" wide metallic gold sheer ribbon with gold edges
1 mixed silk floral candle ring with a 3" wide base, containing 1½"-3" wide ivory-to-dark yellow varieties of rose, magnolia, hydrangea, ranunculus, gardenia and iris blossoms and many various leaves
1 green plastic candle spike for a taper candle
10" white taper candle
small handful of green sheet moss
U-shaped floral pins
24-gauge wire, wire cutters
low temperature glue gun, glue sticks

Helpful Hint

Because this pot is lightweight and can tip easily, set it in an area where it won't be bumped. To avoid this, substitute a 4"x4"x5½" painted terra cotta pot in its place.

---

1 **For the base:** glue the candle spike centered on the foam top. Glue moss to cover the foam.

2 Cut the ribbon in half. Use each length to make a puffy bow (see page 9) with three 2" loops, one 6" tail and one 7" tail. Glue the bows to the candle ring on opposite sides. Place the candle ring onto the floral pot and secure it with the floral pins and glue. Insert the candle into the holder.

Floral Ivy Bowl
by Kathy Thompson

4"x4"x5" clear glass ivy bowl
2 yards of ¾" wide metallic gold sheer
ribbon with gold edges
1 mixed silk floral candle ring with a
3" wide plastic base, containing 1½"-
3" wide ivory-to-dark yellow rose,
magnolia, hydrangea, ranunculus,
gardenia and iris blossoms, many
various leaves
1 green plastic candle spike for a taper
candle
10" white taper candle
⅛ oz. of green sheet moss
E6000® glue
24-gauge wire, wire cutters
low temperature glue gun,
glue sticks

Designer Tip
For added impact, fill the bowl with water and fresh lemon slices.

1 **For the base:** use wire cutters to clip the spike from the bottom of the plastic candle spike. Working in a well-ventilated area, use the E6000® glue to adhere the candle spike to the inside center base of the ivy bowl. Let it dry overnight.

2 **Ribbon**—cut it into four 18" lengths. Tie each length into a shoestring bow (see page 9) with two 2" loops and two 2" tails. Glue the bows evenly spaced on the candle ring, with the loops and tails extending upward. Set the ivy bowl inside the center of the candle ring and add the candle.

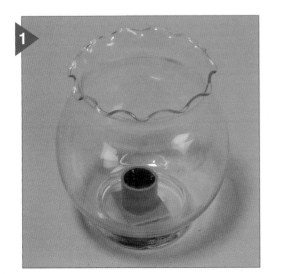

Reception Decorations

Wreath Votive
by LeNae Gerig

2½"x2" clear glass votive cup
3½" wide twig wreath with a 2" wide opening
eight ¾" wide pink silk mini flowers with two ¼"
*   wide clusters of pink berries, two 1" long leaves*
three ¾" wide blue silk mini flowers with two 1"
*   long leaves*
four ¾" wide white silk mini flowers with ¼"
*   wide cluster of white berries, two 1" long leaves*
tea light candle
low temperature glue gun, glue sticks

Place the votive cup in the wreath center with the candle inside. Glue the flowers to the wreath, alternating the colors. Glue the berry clusters and leaves evenly spaced among the flowers.

Flower Pot Votive
by LeNae Gerig

2¾"x2¾" clear glass flower pot votive cup
15" of ½" wide white satin ribbon
six 8mm white flat-backed pearls
white votive candle
tacky craft glue

Glue the ribbon center to the back of the votive rim. Wrap it around to the front and tie the ends into a shoestring bow (see page 9) with 1" loops and tails. Trim each ribbon tail end into an inverted "V". **Pearls**—glue the halves evenly spaced around the lower half of the cup. Place the candle inside the votive.

Burgundy Votive
by LeNae Gerig

3"x3" ribbed clear glass ivy bowl
18" length of ½" wide burgundy wire-edged ribbon
¾" wide burgundy silk rosebud with three ½" long
  leaves
4" of 2mm white fused pearls
tea light candle
low temperature glue gun, glue sticks

Wrap the ribbon around the bowl's neck and tie it in a shoestring bow (see page 9) with two 1" loops and two 2" tails. Glue the rosebud onto the center of the bow. Fold the pearls in half and glue the fold under the bud. Place the candle inside the votive.

Floating Candle Votive
by LeNae Gerig

5¼"x5¼" clear glass ribbed ivy bowl
7" wide silk floral candle ring with 3" wide base, 1"
  wide ivory roses, 1½"-2" leaves, clusters of 2" wide
  silk baby's breath sprigs
½ oz. white preserved baby's breath
15" of 4mm white fused pearls
15" of ½" wide white sheer ribbon with white satin
  edges
eight 8mm white flat-backed pearls
3" wide white floral floating candle
water
tacky craft glue

Place the ivy bowl in the candle ring center. **Baby's breath**—cut to 1"-2" sprigs and glue them evenly among the roses and leaves. **Pearls**—weave them among the roses, gluing every 3". Tie the ribbon around the bowl's neck. Glue the pearl halves evenly spaced onto the upper portion of the bowl. **Finishing touch**—fill the bowl ⅔ full with water, place the candle in the water and light it just before the guests arrive.

Reception Decorations

Cake Toppers
by Kathy Thompson

Cake shown with top, a medium topper on the center tier and three sets of the medium and small toppers around the base.

For one set of toppers:

2 yards of ⅞" wide pink/green rainbow ribbon with wired edges

4 silk floral taper candle rings, each with one 2" wide yellow rose, one 2" wide white rose, one 3" cluster of green/burgundy hydrangea blossoms, one 3" cluster of pink/white hydrangea blossoms, nine 1¾" leaves

1 green variegated silk bush, with three 6" sprigs, one 8" sprig and one 11" sprig, each with many ¾"-1½" leaves

½ oz. of green preserved plumosus fern

low temperature glue gun, glue sticks

24-gauge wire, wire cutters

1 **Ivy**—cut the sprigs off the bush and set them aside for steps 2-4. **Ribbon**—cut two 18" lengths. Fold one length to make a center 3" loop with two 5" tails; secure with wire. Repeat for the other length. Use the remaining ribbon to make a puffy bow (see page 9) with three 2½" loops and two 7" tails. Set each bow aside for steps 2-4.

2 **For the cake top:** cut the white and yellow rose from one candle ring, then place the second ring under the first with the opposite hydrangea clusters meeting; wire them together. Wire the white and yellow rose back onto the ring as shown. **Ivy sprigs**—weave the 11" sprig around the candle ring and secure with wire. Wire the 6" sprigs to the ring, one on each side. **Puffy bow**—glue it to the candle ring center, so the tails extend outward along the 6" ivy sprigs. **Fern**—cut and glue 12 sprigs evenly spaced among the blossoms and bow loops.

3 **Medium topper:** pinch the candle ring in half so the hydrangea clusters meet and wire to secure. **8" ivy**—wire it to the candle ring, extending out from under each hydrangea cluster. **Ribbon loop**—glue one centered between the roses, with the tails extending outward along the ivy sprigs. **Fern**—glue eight sprigs evenly spaced among the blossoms and ribbon.

4 **Small topper:** wire the remaining ivy sprig to the candle ring, centered between the roses, with the ends extending outward. **Ribbon loop**—glue the remaing bow centered between the roses, with the tails extending outward along the ivy sprigs. **Fern**—glue eight sprigs evenly spaced around the blossoms and ribbon. Place the medium and small toppers around the cake base, so the ribbon ends touch alternating the sizes.

Cake Top & Floral Clusters
by Kathy Thompson

*1⅔ yards of 1½" wide dark blue sheer ribbon
    with gold wired edges
2 stems of green silk hibiscus leaves, each with
    eight 3"-4" wide leaves
1 burgundy silk peony stem with a 5" wide
    blossom and three 2½"-3½" leaf sprigs
1 plum silk rose stem with one 4" wide blossom, a
    3-leaf and a 5-leaf sprig
1 burgundy silk rose stem with three 1½"-3" wide
    blossoms, a closed bud and five leaf sprigs
four 2" wide natural dried pomegranates
five 2" wide clusters of yellow dried yarrow
2 oz. of preserved eucalyptus sprigs
low temperature glue gun, glue sticks
green floral tape*

1 **Hibiscus leaf bases:** Cut each stem to 1". Stack six leaves together for the large topper, all right side up. Twist the stems together and tape to secure. Form the leaves in a circular pattern, with one extending upward in the center; bend the stem back so the base lies flat. Repeat to make two 4-leaf bases and one 2-leaf base, all without the upright leaf.

2 **For the cake top:** cut each peony and rose blossom from the stems. Glue one on each side of the upright leaf on the 6-leaf base. **Ribbon**—cut two 18" lengths. Form each into a single 4" loop with two 5" tails; trim each end in an inverted "V". Glue one on each side of the blossoms, extending the tails outward. **Pomegranates**— glue one beside each center loop of each bow. **Rose leaves**—cut two 1-leaf and three 2-leaf sprigs. Glue them evenly spaced among the materials. **Yarrow**—cut into 21 smaller clusters and set 15 aside for Steps 3 and 4. Glue six clusters evenly spaced among the blossoms and leaves. Cut eight 4" eucalyptus sprigs; glue them evenly spaced angled upward and outward.

3 **For the two 4-leaf clusters:** cut each burgundy rose blossom and leaf from the stem. Glue one blossom and a pomegranate together on the center of a 4-leaf base. Glue five rose leaves evenly spaced around the rose blossom. **Ribbon**— cut four 4" lengths and cut an inverted "V" into one end of each. Glue one to each side of the rose, rippling the tails outward on each base. Cut twelve 3" eucalyptus sprigs; glue six yarrow and six eucalyptus sprigs evenly spaced on each base as shown.

4 **For the 2-leaf topper:** Glue the burgundy rosebud to the base center. Glue three rose leaves evenly spaced around the bud blossom. Cut two 4" ribbon lengths and cut an inverted "V" into one end of each. Glue one on each side of the rose, rippling the tails outward. Cut three 3" eucalyptus sprigs; glue three yarrow and three eucalyptus sprigs around the rose as shown.

Reception Decorations

Pink & White Cake Topper
by LeNae Gerig

1¾"x4½" clear acrylic cake top base
4"x6" clear arcylic lovebirds cake pick
7½" pink tulle floral pick with six 1½" wide flowers with pearl
    centers, 1½" leaves and twelve 2½"pearl sprays
7½" white tulle floral pick with six 1½" wide white flowers
    with pearl centers, 1½" leaves and twelve 2½" pearl sprays
7½" white tulle floral pick with six 1¼" wide white flowers
    with pearl centers and 1½" leaves
8" white tulle/pearlescent floral pick, with 2" wide flowers with
    pearl centers and 12 pearl sprays
7" white silk floral pick, with six 4" sprigs of 1¼"wide blossoms
    with pearl centers
18" of ⅛" wide pink satin ribbon
2" white foam ball, serrated knife
26-gauge wire, wire cutters
low temperature glue gun, glue sticks

1 Use the serrated knife to cut the foam ball in half. Glue the flat side of a ball half centered on the
cake top base. Insert the lovebirds into the foam center. **8" pick**—cut the stem to 7" and fan out
the blossoms. Insert it into the foam, behind the lovebirds.

2 **7" pick**—cut the 4" sprigs from the stem and insert them fanned out in front of the lovebirds.
Pink floral pick—cut the stem to three 4" and three 2" sprigs. Insert the taller sprigs evenly
spaced among the taller white blossoms and the 2" sprigs fanned out near the front edge of the foam.
Remaining floral picks—cut the stems to 1"-2" sprigs. Insert them evenly spaced into the foam to fill empty areas.
Ribbon—make a loopy bow (see page 9) with six 2" loops and no tails; secure the bow with wire, leaving a 1" wire tail.
Insert the bow wire into the foam at the lower right.

Double Ring Cake Topper
by LeNae Gerig

6½"x4½" white double ring cake top with doves and tulle
eight ¾" wide burgundy silk flowers, each with three ¼" wide
    berry clusters and 1" leaves
18" of ⅛" wide burgundy satin ribbon
1" wide white plastic dove
26-gauge wire, wire cutters
low temperature glue gun, glue sticks

Cut the stems of the flowers to 1"-2". Glue the longer sprigs
to the center back of the base and the shorter sprigs near the
front. With the ribbon, make a loopy bow (see page 9) with
four 1½" loops and two 3" tails. Glue the bow in front of
the flowers near the lower right. Glue the dove to the bow
center.

Pink & White Serving Set
by LeNae Gerig

two 1¼" wide pink tulle flowers, each with a ¼"
  wide pink ribbon rose center
1½ yards of ⅛" wide pink satin ribbon
10" of 3mm white fused pearls
22-gauge wire, wire cutters
tacky craft glue
low temperature glue gun, glue sticks

Cut the ribbon in half. Use each length to make
a loopy bow (see page 9) with four 2" loops and
two 5" tails. Cut the blossoms from the stems.
Glue one to the center of each bow. **Pearls**—cut
the strand in half. Fold each in half, staggering the
ends; glue to the bottom back of each blossom.
Attach the bows to the serving pieces as described
in the tip box below.

Designer Tip

*Use tacky craft glue to attach the bows to the knife, server handles and glasses. Wrap the bow tails
around the back and tie them together. The tacky glue will help secure the bows in place, but will
wash off easily after the reception.*

Ivory Toasting Set
by LeNae Gerig

two 2" wide ivory satin and silk flowers, each
  with a pearl center
1½ yards of ⅛" wide ivory satin ribbon
22-gauge wire, wire cutters
tacky craft glue
low temperature glue gun, glue sticks

Cut the ribbon in half. Use each length to make
a loopy bow (see page 9) with four 2" loops and
two 5" tails. Cut the blossoms from the stems
and glue one to the center of each bow. Attach
the bows to the glasses as described in the tip
box above.

Tips

W e know it can be a bit daunting to identify silk florals, so we've provided product shots throughout the book. Below are some extras to help you identify just what you'll need. In most cases, we've used the common names of flowers and plants. You'll find nearly all supplies used throughout this book at your local craft store.

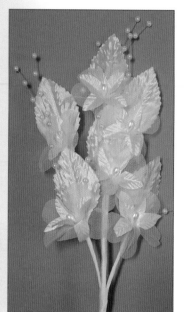

floral pick with satin leaves

ivory silk magnolia blossoms

green plumosus fern

green silk hibiscus leaves

white silk peony

white silk gypsophilia

white tulle flowers with pearls

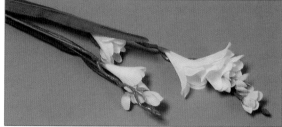

white silk freesia

pink silk delphinium

white satin starflower pick

green preserved eucalyptus

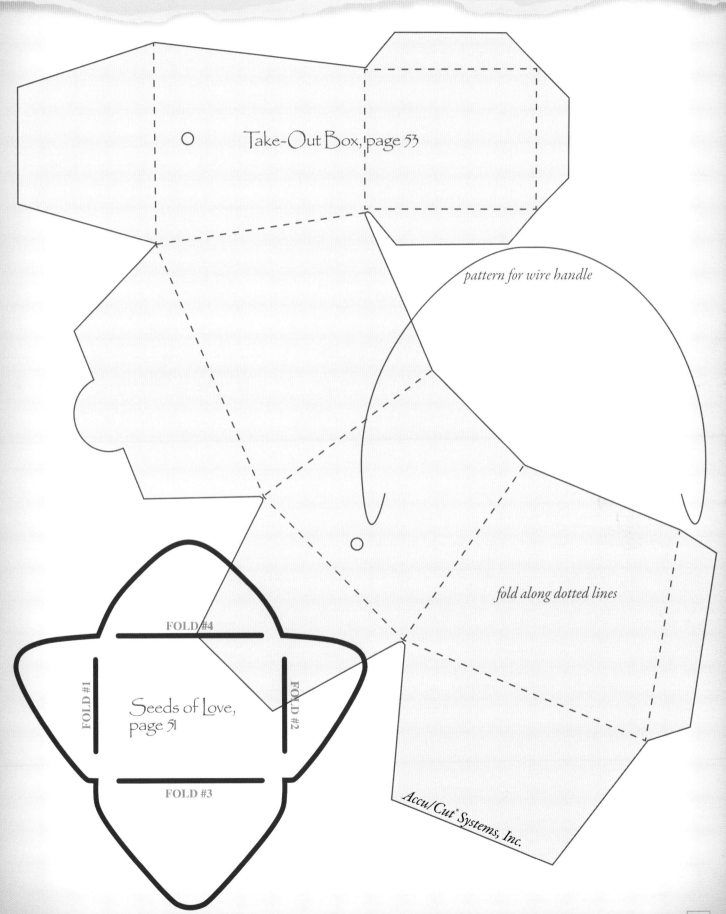

Take-Out Box, page 53

pattern for wire handle

fold along dotted lines

FOLD #4

FOLD #1

FOLD #2

Seeds of Love,
page 51

FOLD #3

Accu/Cut® Systems, Inc.

Patterns

fold along dotted lines

Paper Box, page 52

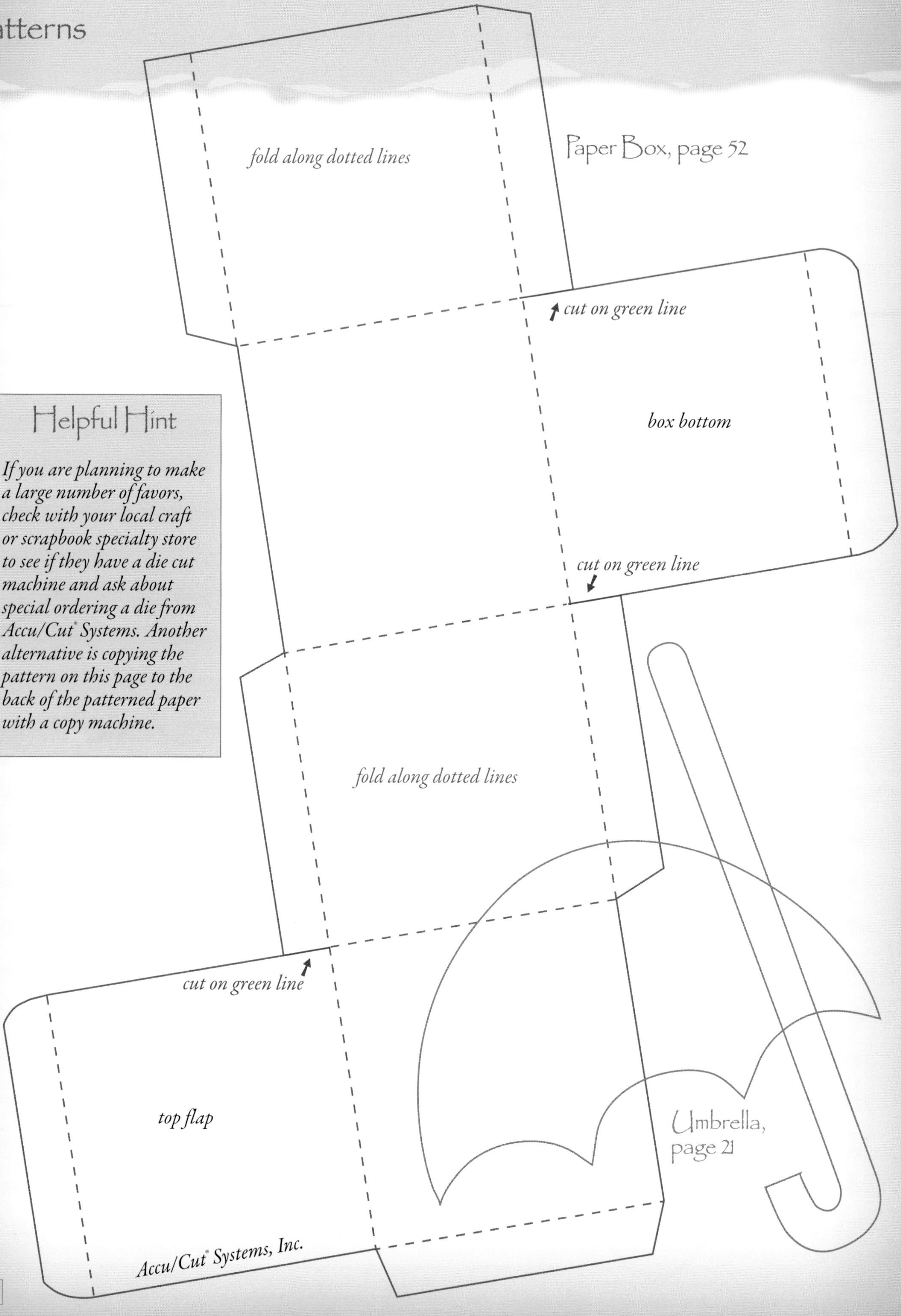

↑ *cut on green line*

box bottom

cut on green line ↘

Helpful Hint

If you are planning to make a large number of favors, check with your local craft or scrapbook specialty store to see if they have a die cut machine and ask about special ordering a die from Accu/Cut® Systems. Another alternative is copying the pattern on this page to the back of the patterned paper with a copy machine.

fold along dotted lines

cut on green line ↑

top flap

Umbrella, page 21

Accu/Cut® Systems, Inc.

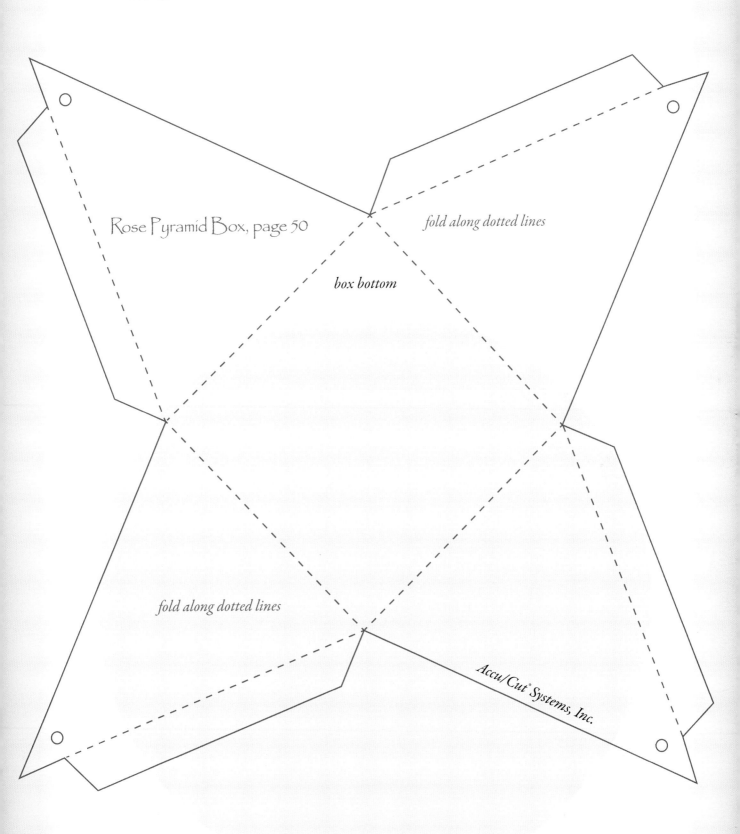

Rose Pyramid Box, page 50

fold along dotted lines

box bottom

fold along dotted lines

Accu/Cut® Systems, Inc.

Vellum Cone, page 50

Manufacturers & Suppliers

Accu/Cut® Systems, Inc.
(die cuts)
1035 E. Dodge Street
Fremont, NE 68025
www.accucut.com

Adhesive Technologies, Inc.
(craft glue, low temperature glue guns, glue sticks)
3 Merrill Industrial Drive
Hampton, NH 03842
www.adhesivetech.com

Allstate Floral & Craft, Inc.
(silk flowers, silk greenery)
14038 Park Place
Cerritos, CA 90703
www.allstatefloral.com

Anchor Hocking
(bud vase, ivy bowls, pillar candle dish, storage jars, votive cups)
519 Pierce Avenue
Lancaster, OH 43130
www.anchorhocking.com

C.M. Offray & Son, Inc.
(Lion Ribbon Co.)
(ribbon, satin ribbon roses)
360 Route 24, Box 601
Chester, NJ 07930
www.offray.com

Creative Beginnings
(gold charms)
475 Morro Bay Boulevard
Morro Bay, CA 93442
www.creativebeginnings.com

Darice, Inc.
(battery candlestick, bird nests, candleholders, flat-backed pearls, floating candles, floral candle rings, floral tape, ivory heart-shape pillow, plastic headbands, satin-covered headbands, silk floral bushes, silk flowers, silk greenery, silk vines, veils, votive cups, willow baskets, wire)
13000 Darice Parkway
Strongsville, OH 44149
www.darice.com

Decorator & Craft Corporation
(papier mâché boxes)
428 S. Zelta
Wichita, KS 67207

Ellison Craft & Design
(umbrella die cut)
25862 Commercentre Drive
Lake Forest, CA 92630

Eclectic Products, Inc.
(E6000® glue)
995 South A Street
Springfield, OR 97477

EK Success, Ltd.
(Zig® pens)
125 Entin Road
Clifton, NJ 07014
www.eksuccess.com

Family Treasures, Inc.
(paper punches, pattern-edged scissors)
24922 Anza Dr., Unit A
Valencia, CA 91355
www.familytreasures.com

Fiskars®
(hole punches, pattern- and straight-edged scissors)
7811 W. Stewart Avenue
Wausau, WI 54401
www.fiskars.com

FloraCraft Corporation
(cherub planters, white resin urn)
One Longfellow Place
Ludington, MI 49431
www.floracraft.com

Hirschberg Schutz & Co., Inc.
(acrylic champagne glass, acrylic slipper, acrylic swan, bubbles, flower clusters, gold bells, hair combs, lace appliques, paper roses, pearl headpieces, plastic headbands, ribbon, ribbon roses, satin flowers, satin headbands, tulle, veils, white basket)
650 Liberty Avenue
Union, NJ 07083

Hot Off The Press, Inc.
(blank cards, envelope templates, patterned and vellum papers)
1250 NW Third, Dept. B
Canby, OR 97013
www.paperwishes.com

Indiana Glass
(glass candlesticks, ivy bowls, vases)
P.O. Box 42364
Cinncinnati, OH 45242

InkADinkADo, Inc.
(rubber stamps)
61 Holton Street
Woburn, MA 01801

Krylon®
(metallic spray paint, sealer, spray paint, textured paint)
31500 Solon Road
Solon, OH 44139
www.krylon.com

Marvy® Uchida
(Uchida of America Corp.)
(pens, punches)
3535 Del Amo Blvd.
Torrance, CA 90503
www.uchida.com

Paper Flair™
(see Hot Off The Press, Inc.)

Paper Pizazz®
(see Hot Off The Press, Inc.)

Pentel of America, Ltd.
(pens)
2805 Columbia St.
Torrance, CA 90509

Pioneer Photo Albums, Inc.
(guest books, photo album)
9801 Deering Avenue
Chatsworth, CA 91311
www.pioneerphotoalbums.com

Rubber Stampede
(rubber stamps)
2550 Pellissier Place
Whittier, CA 90601
www.deltacrafts.com

Schusters of Texas, Inc.
(bird, butterflies, dried and preserved greenery, grapevines, honeysuckle vines, sheet moss)
2109 Priddy Road
Goldthwaite, TX 76844
www.schustersoftexas.com

Smithers-Oasis, U.S.A.
(bouquet holders, candle spikes, floral foam, foam flower pot, wrist corsage bands, pew clips)
919 Marvin Avenue
Kent, OH 44240
www.smithersoasis.com

Wilton Enterprises
(cake top bases, heart cake pick, rhinestone tiara)
2240 West 75th Street
Woodridge, IL 60517
www.wilton.com